Integrating Spirituality Into Multicultural Counseling

MULTICULTURAL ASPECTS OF COUNSELING SERIES

SERIES EDITOR

Paul Pedersen, Ph.D., *University of Alabama at Birmingham*

VOLUMES IN THIS SERIES

1. **Increasing Multicultural Understanding (2nd edition): A Comprehensive Model**
   by Don C. Locke
2. **Preventing Prejudice: A Guide for Counselors and Educators**
   by Joseph G. Ponterotto and Paul B. Pedersen
3. **Improving Intercultural Interactions: Modules for Cross-Cultural Training Programs**
   edited by Richard W. Brislin and Tomoko Yoshida
4. **Assessing and Treating Culturally Diverse Clients (2nd edition): A Practical Guide**
   by Freddy A. Paniagua
5. **Overcoming Unintentional Racism in Counseling and Therapy: A Practitioner's Guide to Intentional Intervention**
   by Charles R. Ridley
6. **Multicultural Counseling With Teenage Fathers: A Practical Guide**
   by Mark S. Kiselica
7. **Multicultural Counseling Competencies: Assessment, Education and Training, and Supervision**
   edited by Donald B. Pope-Davis and Hardin L. K. Coleman
8. **Improving Intercultural Interactions: Modules for Cross-Cultural Training Programs, Volume 2**
   edited by Kenneth Cushner and Richard W. Brislin
9. **Understanding Cultural Identity in Intervention and Assessment**
   by Richard H. Dana
10. **Psychological Testing of American Minorities (2nd edition)**
    by Ronald J. Samuda
11. **Multicultural Counseling Competencies: Individual and Organizational Development**
    by Derald Wing Sue et al.
12. **Counseling Multiracial Families**
    by Bea Wehrly, Kelly R. Kenney, and Mark E. Kenney
13. **Integrating Spirituality Into Multicultural Counseling**
    by Mary A. Fukuyama and Todd D. Sevig
14. **Counseling With Native American Indians and Alaska Natives: Strategies for Helping Professionals**
    by Roger D. Herring

Integrating Spirituality Into Multicultural Counseling

Mary A. Fukuyama
Todd D. Sevig

Multicultural Aspects of Counseling Series 13

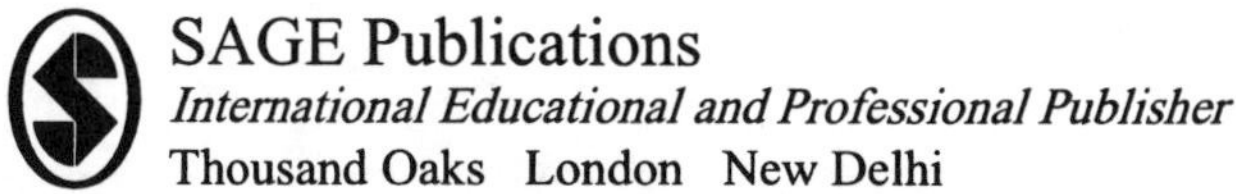

SAGE Publications
International Educational and Professional Publisher
Thousand Oaks London New Delhi

For information:

SAGE Publications, Inc.
2455 Teller Road
Thousand Oaks, California 91320
E-mail: order@sagepub.com

SAGE Publications Ltd.
6 Bonhill Street
London EC2A 4PU
United Kingdom

SAGE Publications India Pvt. Ltd.
M-32 Market
Greater Kailash I
New Delhi 110 048 India

Printed in the United States of America

Library of Congress Cataloging-in-Publication Data

Fukuyama, Mary A.
Integrating spirituality into multicultural counseling / by Mary A. Fukuyama, Todd D. Sevig.
p. cm.—(Multicultural aspects of counseling series; v. 13)
Includes bibliographical references.
ISBN 0-7619-1583-4 (cloth: alk. paper)
ISBN 0-7619-1584-2 (pbk.: alk. paper)
1. Cross-cultural counseling. 2. Spirituality. 3. Pluralism (Social Sciences)—Religious aspects. 4. Transpersonal psychology. 5. Religion and culture. I. Sevig, Todd D. II. Title. III. Series.
BF637 .C6 F795 1999
158′.3—dc21 99-6397

This book is printed on acid-free paper.

99 00 01 02 03 04 05 7 6 5 4 3 2 1

Acquiring Editor: Kassie Gavrilis
Editorial Assistant: Heidi Van Middlesworth
Production Editor: Wendy Westgate
Editorial Assistant: Nevair Kabakian
Typesetter: Lynn Miyata
Cover Designer: Candice Harman

Contents

Series Editor's Introduction

Integrating spiritual issues into multicultural counseling is a topic of rapidly growing importance among counselors. The professional meeting sessions on spiritual issues are typically crowded, with standing room only, and there are many publications coming out just in the past few years. This spiritual revival among counselors is long overdue. We already know that while spiritual/religious issues are important to about 75% of our clients, those same spiritual issues are important to about 40% of the counselors working with those clients. This difference must be addressed if counselors are to understand the spiritual contexts of their clients, particularly of their culturally different clients. For that reason this volume on spiritual issues is extremely appropriate for The Multicultural Aspects of Counseling book series.

Fukuyama and Sevig have condensed their lifetime interest in spiritual issues into this small volume, which will open doors and admit the fresh breezes of new knowledge for readers. In many cultures the only questions worth asking are about what happened before birth and what will happen after death. Those topics are glaringly absent in most books about counseling and would not be considered appropriate in many, if not most, counselor education classes. That pattern is changing because our clients are demanding that it be changed. Our clients have less and less tolerance for counselors who lack, or even avoid discussing, the important spiritual resources on which clients typically depend. The topic of spirituality is extremely relevant and offers counselors an opportunity to "catch up" with their clients.

Fukuyama and Sevig use the metaphor of a "spiritual journey" to describe the experience readers can expect to encounter as they proceed through this book. This conceptual framework of a journey is applied to a variety of cultures, such as those of Native American Indians and African Americans, but the framework works just as well for many other cultural groups. The interaction of multicultural competence and the spiritual perspective is highlighted in practical ways that help readers understand the connection between Spirit and Culture.

Hard questions about positive and negative expressions of spirituality are addressed directly in a controversial conversation between Fukuyama and Sevig, and the reader. They present a very realistic perspective toward questions like, "What is healthy spirituality?" "What is unhealthy spirituality?" and "What distinguishes healthy and/or unhealthy spirituality?" This conversational writing style comes through as a very personal encounter with the authors on topics that are often considered very private and sensitive. Even when you disagree with the authors, you will learn more about your own spiritual views in the process of disagreeing.

Fukuyama and Sevig also focus on content issues such as death and dying, working with clients who are near death, and generating a culturally appropriate response to death in a variety of different cultural contexts. Other content issues focus on power, control and empowerment, sexual power, work power, creativity, and healing. We know that 80% of the world's population depends on Alternative and Complementary therapies for health and healing; 75% of the European population and more than 50% of the U.S. population, as well, depend on Alternative therapies. The spiritual content issues are closely related to understanding and interpreting those Alternative and Complementary therapies.

Process issues such as the role of counselors and clients, and the interaction of clients and counselors in ethical ways on the topic of spirituality are also addressed. The contraindications and cautions identified by Fukuyama and Sevig give the reader a very realistic perspective. The final issue in the book is an examination of spiritual interventions and an "integrative" model. The process is as important as the content in appropriately addressing spiritual issues through counseling.

This book is realistic in its emphasis, right from the opening parable that points out that anyone who claims to know how to purify your thoughts is a fake! This book is practical, identifying specific guidelines for managing spiritual issues in counseling. This book is comprehensive, looking at spiritual issues from a variety of cultural perspectives. This book is current, preparing the competent counselor for work with clients whose spiritual awareness is rapidly increasing.

—Paul Pedersen
University of Alabama at Birmingham

Preface

> A disciple came to the celebrated Master of the Good Name with a question. "Rabbi, how are we to distinguish between a true master and a fake?"
>
> And the Master of the Good Name said, "when you meet a person who poses as a master, ask him [*sic*] a question: Whether he knows how to purify your thoughts. If he says that he knows, then he is a fake."
>
> In other words, anyone who tells you that he has the answers to the questions—with all apologies to your teachers—don't believe him. There are no answers to true questions. There are only good questions, painful sometimes, exuberant at others. Whatever I have learned in my life is questions, and whatever I have tried to share with friends is questions.
>
> —Elie Wiesel, *"Whatever I Have Learned in My Life Is Questions"* (1974, p. 276)

This book represents a 10-year professional quest by the coauthors to integrate spirituality into multicultural counseling. As mental health professionals and educators, we have sensed the importance of recognizing spirituality in the context of a multicultural world. One of the challenges in writing this book is that there are no certain answers. We have begun with this Elie Wiesel quote precisely because the best we can do is to identify and explore good questions. We urge you, the reader, to do the same.

One of the difficulties in articulating spiritual meanings and processes is that we are analyzing things that are highly personal, subjective, emotional, and dynamic, meaning that it is possible that by putting these concepts into words, we will miss out on what we seek most. By codifying and making spiritual experiences concrete, we may unintentionally restrict or truncate the experience.

Our highest hope is that we provide a psychologically based guide to understanding spiritual issues that may be present in multicultural counseling and multicultural learning processes. We intend to stimulate your curiosity and inspire you to seek answers to your own questions on these issues. We will share insights that we have gained through talking with clients, teaching graduate and undergraduate students, sharing with colleagues, and doing professional educational workshops on this topic. We are grateful to every one of these people for their personal sharing, which has given us a broader understanding of spiritual concerns and processes.

This book is written to a broadly defined audience of mental health professionals, primarily those engaged in the counseling process in clinical work. It is also appropriate for graduate counseling training. The book is written in a sequence that will guide the reader through self-awareness exercises to expand a personal understanding of multiple views of spirituality and its interaction with multicultural counseling processes.

Just as the definitions and understandings related to multiculturalism shift from year to year, we imagine that the spiritual insights of today will look different tomorrow. Considering the rapid changes in postmodern society, it is difficult to predict what direction this will all take. Suffice it to say that this book is a "work in progress," and we hope it will stimulate further investigation of the subject.

In the first chapter, introductory comments and definitions will be discussed. Self-reflection questions are included for the reader to assess his or her personal awareness of spirituality, religion, and multicultural concepts.

In Chapter 2, the spiritual journey will be introduced by examining the universals of religion and spirituality, and through exploring culture-specific worldviews of Native American spirituality, Afrocentric spirituality, and women's spirituality.

In Chapter 3, the spiritual journey will be explored through examination of developmental models of faith, optimal identity, and stages of mysticism that are found throughout the life span.

In Chapter 4, the similarities between multicultural learning processes and spiritual evolvement will be noted. One of our central theses is that approaching multiculturalism from a spiritual perspective will enhance multicultural learning processes. Conversely, engaging in multicultural processes may be a source of intentional spiritual growth. Similarly, the acquisition of spiritual and multicultural competencies may be complementary to each other.

Chapter 5 focuses on the question, "What is healthy or unhealthy spirituality?" This question is related directly to many concerns that counselors and psychologists have due to a long history of distrust of religion by mental health professionals.

Chapters 6 and 7 explore content issues in counseling that are existential in nature. Although many issues might fit this criterion, we have selected areas that are connected to spirituality through negativity (loss, pain) and through positivity (empowerment, creativity). Chapter 6 focuses on spiritual concerns that arise out of suffering and coping with death. Chapter 7 explores empowerment and creative processes as related to spirituality. Clinical case examples are included (with details changed to protect the anonymity of clients).

Chapter 8 explores counseling process issues related to addressing spiritual issues in counseling, including ethics and contraindications.

We conclude the book in Chapter 9 with the introduction of an integrative model that interweaves spirituality, psychological growth, and multiculturalism. Spiritual interventions are reviewed, but rather than provide a "cookbook" for spiritual interventions, we outline principles for ongoing professional and personal development in this area. Just as multicultural learning is a lifetime process, integrating spirituality into multicultural counseling is a lifelong journey.

A repeating theme throughout the multicultural literature is that Western empiricism has compartmentalized many aspects of life in order to study them. Yet by reducing life to quantifiable units, it is easy to lose track of the connectedness of these pieces, or of the big picture. In the course of this book, many issues are identified and discussed in a somewhat segmented style. For this we apologize. However, we invite you to use these ideas as a springboard for further exploration and expanded understanding of what it means to integrate spirituality into multicultural counseling.

—Mary A. Fukuyama and Todd D. Sevig
December 21, 1998

Reference

Wiesel, E. (1974). Whatever I have learned in my life is questions. In A. Chapman (Ed.), *Jewish-American literature: An anthology* (pp. 276-278). New York: Mentor New American Library.

Acknowledgments

I would like to thank the many people, both named and unnamed, who have contributed and continue to contribute to my growth and understanding of the intersection of counseling, culture, and spirit. It is truly a spiritual journey and quite a caravan of fellow travelers. In particular, I would like to thank my partner Jackie Davis for ongoing support and encouragement, Deb Ramsey for endless computer assistance, Ed Delgado-Romero and Robin Rompre for reading early drafts, Annie Pais for believing in the artist in me, my colleagues at the University of Florida Counseling Center, and my spiritual community at the United Church of Gainesville. In addition, I appreciate the openness of the many clients and students I have been privileged to know, who have shared their stories and thereby enriched me. I am also grateful for the guidance of many culturally diverse spiritual teachers who continue to shape my journey.

—M.A.F.

I would like to thank the many people who have shared a conversation or two with me about the topics in the following pages—these interactions provide the rhythm of my life and, in some fashion, are in this book. Specifically, I would like to thank, first and foremost, my wife Sharon

Vaughters, who continues to believe in me. I would also like to thank my colleagues past and present at Counseling & Psychological Services and the Program on Intergroup Relations, Conflict, & Community, both at the University of Michigan. Finally, I would like to thank the many clients and students I have interacted with—I value the work we have shared.

—T.D.S.

In loving memory of my parents,
Tsutomu Tom and Betty Adkins Fukuyama, who,
through their courage to enter into an interracial,
intercultural marriage, modeled a pioneering
spirit and vision for a pluralistic world.
My father's work as a minister and spiritual leader
and my mother's work as a poet and artist
have given me inspiration for this book.

—M.A.F.

To my father, Palmer, and
in loving memory of my mother, Shirley Sevig,
who continue to grant me a sense of serenity
and worldly spirituality. Their work—as parents,
and my father's as a minister and my mother's as a
musician and music teacher—stays with me.
To my children, Mara and Joseph—
may your own journeys be filled with wonder.

—T.D.S.

1

Introduction

Every cultural crisis produces a corresponding spiritual crisis.

—Matthew Fox, *On Becoming a Musical Mystical Bear* (1976, p. xxviii)

Rationale and Purpose

With the approach of the 21st century and increasing global linkages through technology and interdependent economies, people's day-to-day lives are affected by interactions with others different from themselves. Examples of cross-cultural contact can be found in the streets of our cities, in the business world, and through technology, such as television and the Internet. The cultural diversity of the United States presents both challenges and resources for solving social problems. Concurrently, there is a resurgence of interest in spiritual fulfillment, as participation in fundamentalist churches and in new age activities increases (Hoge, 1996; Naisbett & Aburdene, 1990). Consequently, mental health professionals are asked to learn multicultural competencies (Sue, Arredondo, & McDavis, 1992) and to recognize spiritual issues in counseling (Burke & Miranti, 1995).

The dominant culture in the United States of America is preoccupied with desires for materialism and pleasure. The values of individualism, competition, and independence engender greater isolation of people from each another. As a society, we struggle with many addictions: drugs, food, sex, and relationships (Schaef, 1987). In addition, modern technology is based upon speed and efficiency. With rapid cultural change and the evolution of the information age, it is evident that this society is experiencing both a cultural and a spiritual crisis. We, the authors, however, believe that joining these two phenomena (spirituality and multiculturalism) consciously will yield synergistic results that will ultimately assist the social transformations that are needed in today's world.

In recent years, multicultural issues and spirituality have been addressed in the counseling literature. Multicultural counseling literature has grown exponentially in the past 25 years (see Pedersen, Draguns, Lonner, & Trimble, 1996; Ponterotto, Casas, Suzuki, & Alexander, 1995). Spiritual and religious issues are now formally recognized by the helping professions (Bullis, 1996; Canda, 1998; Cook & Kelly, 1998; Cornett, 1998; Kelly, 1995; Richards & Bergin, 1997; Shafranske, 1996). These recent movements complement the more traditional studies of existential psychology (May & Yalom, 1989), humanistic psychology (Maslow, 1971), transpersonal psychotherapy (Cortright, 1997), psychology and religion (Hood, Spilka, Hunsberger, & Gorsuch, 1996; Wulff, 1997), and pastoral counseling (Clinebell, 1995). With this burgeoning of literature, integral questions become apparent. How do multiculturalism and spirituality interact, and how can they inform each other? This book addresses the intersection of these two forces within the counseling field.

In the 1950s there was a fad in the film industry known as the 3-D movie. Customers wore special glasses to get the effect of three-dimensional imagery from the screen, such that if an ax were thrown at the camera, it would appear to be coming right at the viewer in the audience. This book is not so dramatic (nor so violent), but we propose that counselors don 3-D glasses to examine their professional work through these three forces: counseling, spirituality, and cultural context. We suggest that understanding these three forces in combination will be empowering for clients and stimulating for counselors' personal growth and professional development (see Figure 1.1).

In addition, if the cultural force is made up of several cultures (e.g., a convergence of Asian heritage, North American popular culture, and socioeconomic status), the intersection takes on different nuances. Likewise, spirituality may be expressed in culturally different ways. The counseling orientation and personality of the counselor also shape the inner sphere. Like facets of a diamond, these forces in combination are unique to each counseling situation.

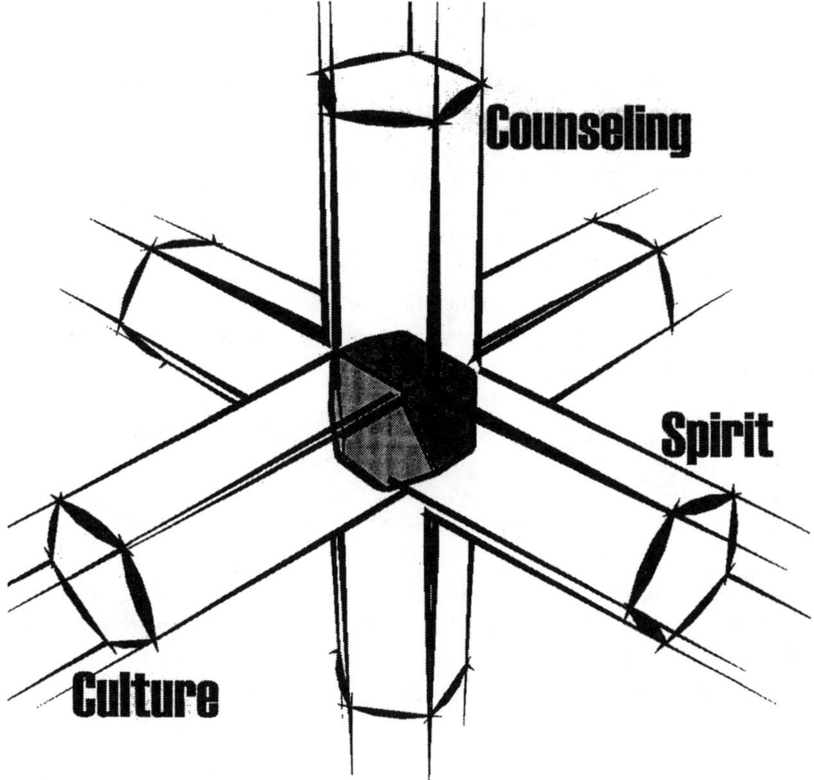

Figure 1.1. The Intersection of Culture, Spirit, and Counseling
NOTE: Graphic by Joel Davis.

These themes will be interwoven throughout the book. These dimensions also highlight and contribute to the increased knowledge, skills, and awareness needed for competent multicultural counseling (Pedersen, 1988).

To meet the purposes of this book, we propose to do the following:

1. Interweave the three strands of spirituality, (multi)culture, and counseling by focusing on the process dimensions of these dynamic forces as they interact with each other
2. Discuss counseling case examples of spiritual issues presented from multicultural perspectives

3. Provide experiential exercises and focus questions for counselor self-awareness and growth on these topics
4. Provide a foundation and springboard that will energize counselors to integrate spirituality into their practice with congruence and synergy

In this chapter, the following topics will be covered:

- definitions of key terms: spirituality, religion, transpersonal, culture, worldview, and multiculturalism
- relevance of spirituality to multicultural counseling
- contemporary contributions toward inclusion of spirituality in counseling
- implications for counselors

Self-reflection exercises will be provided throughout the chapter.

Definitions of Key Terms

The following terms will be discussed briefly in this section: *spirituality, religion, transpersonal, culture, worldview,* and *multiculturalism.* These concepts are complex, however, and these terms are approached in the literature in differing ways. Nevertheless, we have attempted to summarize the essential meanings to meet the purposes of this book.

Spirituality

Discussions within the profession indicate that it is impossible to agree upon only one definition for spirituality (Maher & Hunt, 1993). *Spirituality* is a word that has been used to describe the human need for meaning and value in life and the desire for relationship with a transcendent power (Clinebell, 1995). Spirituality generally refers to something that is transcendent, ultimate, and known in an extrasensory manner (Myers et al., 1991). It is a natural condition for humans to be dissatisfied with self and the world, and to seek transcendence (*transcendere,* from the Latin root, means "to climb over"). Spirituality is a "code word for the depth dimension of human existence" (Becker, as cited in Myers, 1997).

A basic definition of spirituality, from the Latin root *spiritus,* is breath, the essence of life or the life force. Expressed in these terms, spirituality infuses human beings with qualities such as inspiration, creativity, and connection with others. Shafranske and Gorsuch (1984) defined spirituality as the courage to look inside one's self, and as trust and openness to the infinite.

A definition of spirituality developed by leaders of the Association for Spiritual, Ethical, and Religious Values in Counseling (ASERVIC) refers to spirituality as

> the animating force in life, represented by such images as breath, wind, vigor and courage. Spirituality is the infusion and drawing out of spirit in one's life. It is experienced as an active and passive process. It is an innate capacity and tendency to move towards knowledge, love, meaning, hope, transcendence, connectedness and compassion. It includes one's capacity for creativity, growth and the development of a values system. Spirituality encompasses the religious, spiritual and transpersonal. ("Summit Results," 1995)

This definition is useful because it is inclusive, attentive to psychological growth, and fairly compatible with counseling values.

Spirituality may be experienced and expressed through religion, which is characterized by beliefs, social organization, and cumulative traditions. Artress (1995) has suggested that religion is the container and spirituality the essences held within it. Both spirituality and religion have been recognized as important aspects of healing, recovery from addictions, and support during times of human suffering. However, spiritual issues that arise in counseling may or may not be associated with a religious belief system (Ingersoll, 1994).

Definitions of spirituality varied among workshop participants at a national convention on this topic (Forester-Miller, Keel, & Mackie, 1998). The following phrases were gathered from workshop participants, most of whom were professional counselors:

> Remembrance, connection to self and others and universe, relationship to higher source, food for the journey, yearning, space in between the matter, purpose of existence, "here I am" presence, creative force, transformation, expansion, essence, peace, love, joy of Jesus, poetic, inexpressible, sacred in ordinary and extraordinary, felt experience of wholeness, oneness, and grace.

From this list, it can be seen that there are a variety of meanings given to spirituality from both religious and secular origins. A discussion of religion and its contrast to spirituality follows next. (See Box 1.1.)

Box 1.1

Self-Reflection Questions

Recall a time and place that felt spiritual to you. Describe it in detail. What images come to mind when you think of spirituality? Define spirituality for yourself. How is your definition similar or different from those offered above?

Religion

Religion may be defined as an organized system of faith, worship, cumulative traditions, and prescribed rituals (Worthington, 1989). Religion by definition means to "bind together or to express concern" (from the Latin root *religare*). However, the study of religion by psychologists has encompassed a more complex matrix of dimensions, and religion cannot be reduced to a simple construct (Hood et al., 1996).

Religion may be seen as a multidimensional system consisting of six primary components:

1. Ritual: private and/or public ceremonial behavior
2. Doctrine: affirmations about the relationship of the individual to the ultimate
3. Emotion: the presence of feelings (awe, love, fear, etc.)
4. Knowledge: intellectual familiarity with sacred writings and principles
5. Ethics: rules for the guidance of interpersonal behavior, connoting right and wrong, good and bad
6. Community: involvement in a community of the faithful, psychologically, socially, and/or physically (Verbit, as cited in Hood et al., 1996, p. 9)

Each of these components is said to vary along the following four dimensions:

1. Content: the essential nature of the component (e.g., specific rituals, ideas, knowledge, principles, etc.)
2. Frequency: how often the content elements are encountered or are acted upon
3. Intensity: degree of commitment
4. Centrality: importance or salience

Religion and spirituality are expressed in many ways, especially in a culturally diverse nation such as the United States. Religious pluralism has increased through immigration patterns over the past one hundred years (Hoge, 1996), and contemporary figures would place the number of religious groups in the United States at over 2,100 (Creedon, 1998). Changing immigration patterns include increased numbers of Moslems, Catholics (Latin American), and Buddhists, for example. The diversity between and within religious organizations (e.g., mainstream denominations) can be observed in terms of differences between conservative and liberal values and ethnic variations (e.g., African Methodist Episcopal, Latin Catholic, Korean Protestant). Finally, organized religion frequently plays an influential role within local and national politics.

Religion and spirituality are interconnected and we do not propose to separate the two arbitrarily, as that creates unnecessary polarization (Pargament, 1997). The stereotypes of restricting spirituality to the personal and religion to organized groups break down upon closer analysis. That is, although spirituality is thought to be a private, personal matter, spiritual seekers often need to share their experiences with others in some sort of community or group support system. In addition, more and more religious communities are engaged in nurturing spirituality among their constituencies. *Spirituality* as a word is becoming popular, possibly because it fits into a secular and psychologically oriented milieu. Either way, as adjectives, *religious* and *spiritual* describe very similar concepts and processes, and we will frequently use them interchangeably throughout the book. However, they do have different flavors and emphases, and we tend to use the term *spirituality* to represent a universal concept, while *religion* tends to define a more concrete expression.

In this light, we recommend that religion and spirituality be understood in the context of culture. To extend the discussion about universal versus culture-specific approaches to multicultural counseling (Fukuyama, 1990; Locke, 1990), we suggest that spirituality describes universal qualities and religion the culture-specific expressions of spirit. However, religion is paradoxically a culture-specific expression of spirituality AND a transcultural phenomenon. While religion is one of many ways in which culture is embodied and transmitted, it also embodies universal values that transcend cultural boundaries. For example, the Hebrew religion has heritage, language, and rituals that connect people from Ethiopia to New York City (transcultural), yet a 20-year-old Jewish woman in Manhattan may have little in common culturally with a 20-year-old Jewish woman from Addis Ababa, the capital of Ethiopia.

In addition, many world religions have a coherent core belief system, yet are expressed with a variety of cultural nuances; for example, the combined religious customs from Native American traditions and Roman Catholicism in the American Southwest. Religion is woven into cultural identities, ethnicity, and group memberships, and it is a significant contributor to the phenomenon known as ethnocentrism, that is, the belief that one's cultural view is the right one. Although religion has been important for nurturing a spiritual life, increasing numbers of people now are claiming a spirituality outside of organized religion (Chandler, Holden, & Kolander, 1992). The interplay between spirituality and religion will be elaborated in more depth in Chapter 2, which begins the discussion of the spiritual journey.

Transpersonal

Transpersonal refers to "beyond the personal" or "across" the self (from the personal to the transcendent realms). Early proponents of transpersonal psychology were focused on altered states of consciousness. More recent developments include the "melding of the wisdom of the world's spiritual traditions with the learning of modern psychology" (Cortright, 1997, p. 8). Put into other words, "transpersonal psychology is concerned with: developing a self while also honoring the urge to go beyond the self" (p. 9). Strohl (1998) cites Lajoie and Shapiro's definition of transpersonal psychology: "concerned with the study of humanity's highest potential, and with the recognition, understanding, and realization of unitive, spiritual, and transcendent states of consciousness" (p. 397). Transpersonal psychotherapy is concerned with the integration of mind-body-spirit (P. Linn, personal communication, December 23, 1997) and of transcending the limitations of ego identification toward expanded states of awareness (Strohl, 1998). (See Box 1.2.)

Culture

Geertz (1973) suggests that culture consists of a "web of significance" that provides cohesiveness for individuals and groups. Green (1982) adopted a definition that focused on culture "as being made up of those things which are relevant to communication across some kind of social boundary" (p. 7). We prefer to use the following definition for culture, as consisting "of commonalities around which people have developed values, norms, family life-styles, social roles, and behaviors in response to

Box 1.2

Self-Reflection Questions

Religious/Spiritual History

As an introductory personal awareness exercise, we invite you to reflect upon the following questions, adapted from Baldwin (1991). We recommend that you discuss your responses with colleagues with whom you have a trusting relationship.

1. What are some of your earliest memories of religion, church, synagogue, or perhaps absence of religion? What (if any) were your early images of God?
2. What are your earliest memories of nonordinary reality, a higher power, some mystery in the universe, or other spiritual or transpersonal experiences?
3. What were sources of authority, values, and power?
4. What is your experience of transcendence?
5. What resistance or barriers exist that prevent you from connecting with sources of spirituality?
6. Where are you now on your "spiritual journey"?
7. How have your experiences with religion, spirituality, or the transpersonal shaped the attitudes and values that inform your counseling work?

Adapted from Christina Baldwin, *Life's Companion: Journal Writing as a Spiritual Quest* (1991).

historical, political, economic, and social realities" (Christensen, 1989, p. 275). Culture may be viewed as a dynamically changing process that encompasses behaviors, values, and symbols and serves to provide cohesiveness and meaning for group survival.

In the United States of America, multiple cultures coexist, overlap, and sometimes contradict each other. Yet just as the fish does not know it exists in water until it is pulled out, people often are unaware of the culture in which they live until they experience cultural differences.

Worldview

Worldview is a term widely used in the multicultural counseling literature as a way of describing how individuals or groups organize complex cultural information. Worldviews are composed of attitudes, values, opinions, concepts, and philosophies of life construed through the lenses of people's cultural upbringing. Stated more broadly, worldview is "how a person perceives his/her relationship to the world (nature, institutions, other people, etc.)" (Sue & Sue, 1990, p. 137).

Worldview may be explained further by examining the Kluckhohn model for worldviews. Borrowed from anthropological studies, it provides a structure for understanding values and a way to conceptualize spiritual beliefs within a cultural context (Ibrahim, 1985; Kluckhohn & Strodtbeck, 1961). While all cultures have all of the values suggested by this model, different cultures *emphasize* different dimensions of these values, each of which may be construed as existing on a continuum. The five values dimensions found in the Kluckhohn model are

1. human nature (good, bad, mixed, mutable, immutable)
2. relation of humans to nature (subjugated by, in harmony with, mastery over)
3. activity orientation (doing, being, becoming)
4. time orientation (past, present, future)
5. relational (individualistic, collateral group, lineal group)

These dimensions, and in particular the second category of "relation of humans to nature," provide a framework for conceptualizing spiritual beliefs in relation to both the natural and "supernatural" worlds. They can also be used to describe a dimension of "locus of control." The Western-trained counselor is likely to hold a worldview that emphasizes mastery, doing, future-time orientation, and individualism (Katz, 1985). It is important for the multiculturally aware counselor to be able to understand the client's worldview, in particular the client's beliefs around spirituality (i.e., belief in higher power) and his or her relationship to the supernatural or transcendent. For example, in the Santeria tradition, a person might believe that all of life's actions are influenced by gods and goddesses, and that prayers and sacrifices are necessary to ensure harmonious relationships (Gonzalez-Wippler, 1992; Nunez, 1995).

Box 1.3

Self-Reflection Questions

Cultural Baggage

1. Identify your family origins as far back as possible by constructing a family tree or genogram indicating ethnic and national origins.
2. How did your ancestors arrive or where did they originate in this country? Imagine the conditions they experienced. Speculate, if you do not know the details of your family history.
3. Your family's ethnicity and racial background undoubtedly influenced how they were perceived and treated by others. What advantages or disadvantages might they have experienced related to such factors as religious affiliation, economic resources, language, and political involvements.
4. As you reflect upon your family's history, note any strengths, advantages, and privileges that they enjoyed or from which you now benefit.
5. Name your ethnic/cultural background and describe one important personal benefit that you enjoy as a consequence of this identity.
6. Are there residual relational issues between your cultural group and other cultural groups? What are they, and how do you personally experience them?

SOURCE: From J. W. Green, *Cultural Awareness in the Human Services*. Copyright © 1982 by Allyn & Bacon. Adapted by permission.

Multiculturalism

Multiculturalism refers to the recognition of a pluralistic society, one in which many different cultures coexist with equal respect and value. We use the term to include such factors as (a) the ability to "travel" in different cultures; (b) a knowledge of different cultures; (c) personal awareness of one's own cultures and identities; (d) valuing and acting upon multiple perspectives; and (e) acknowledging and acting upon issues of social justice (Zúñiga & Sevig, 1994). (See Box 1.3.)

Relevance of Spirituality to Multicultural Counseling

Both spiritual leaders and counselors have noted the similarity of counseling and spiritual processes. Current counseling literature suggests that spiritual dimensions are important to both client and counselor (Richards & Bergin, 1997). When the general population in the United States is polled, areas such as meaning in life, faith, and religion receive high percentages (Kelly, 1995; Koenig, 1997). When world cultures are considered, "talk therapy" is used by few people when compared to the majority who rely upon religion for meaning and support (Pedersen, 1998). In addition, Pedersen (1998) notes that in terms of numbers, clients tend to be more spiritual or religious than counselors. Student development theory indicates that these are important issues for college students, in particular, as they go through the process of individuation (Fowler, 1981). Finally, spiritual questions of "making meaning" are an appropriate component of cross-cultural existential therapy (Vontress, 1988).

In short, the questions and issues generated from the spiritual dimension are not new—they have been around for a long time. What is new is that the helping professions are starting to recognize the value of incorporating this dimension into counseling and healing. In the past, these areas were not split off. When psychology became a science, however, it divorced itself from religion and that which could not be measured empirically. Now a new paradigm is "reincorporating" the spiritual dimension into counseling practice. Exploring the spiritual dimension within the multicultural context makes implicit sense (Fukuyama & Sevig, 1997; Pate & Bondi, 1992).

Worthington (1989) cited five reasons for counseling psychologists to understand religious faith:

1. A high percentage of Americans consider themselves to be religious.
2. People who are in emotional crisis often spontaneously consider spiritual and religious matters during periods of intense emotions and psychosocial disorganization.

3. Many clients might have religious issues but feel reluctant to bring them up in secular therapy.
4. Therapists are generally more secular than their clients, and this lack of religious orientation may make it more difficult to work maximally with religious clients.
5. This lack of religious knowledge on the part of therapists may result in their missing important aspects of their clients' belief systems.

Spirituality is often an integral component of culture and needs to be addressed by the multiculturally aware counselor. In many cultures, spiritual or religious concerns are not separated from physical, mental, or health concerns. Spiritual forces are believed to be related to illness or psychosocial distress. If we look at the roles of indigenous healers, we are likely to find that a person's symptoms are treated holistically and spiritually. These healers, such as *curanderos* among Mexican Americans (Torres, 1984), folk healers in Asian cultures (Das, 1987; Heinze, 1984; Krippner, 1984), and shamans in Australia (Achterberg, 1985), provide holistic treatment with special attention directed toward the spiritual dimension. Clients who come from such traditional cultural backgrounds are likely to have beliefs that connect spirituality, disease, and healing (Torrey, 1986).

For example, Mexican Americans have a disease named *susto,* or "fright disease," that has the symptoms of anxiety or depression. This disease is thought to be caused by a traumatic experience and to result in the loss of the soul from the body. Treatment might include making "prayers, votive offerings, herbs, and 'sweeping' the patient with a branch by folk healers to draw the soul back" (Torrey, 1986, p. 145).

Spirits also may be called upon to help with healing an illness, such as in the role of the shaman. This ancient healing tradition is described below:

> The shaman, a mystical, priestly, and political figure . . . can be described not only as a specialist in the human soul but also as a generalist whose sacred and social functions can cover an extraordinarily wide range of activities. Shamans are healers, seers, and visionaries who have mastered death. They are in communication with the world of gods and spirits. Their bodies can be left behind while they fly to unearthly realms. They are poets and singers. They dance and create works of art. They are not only spiritual leaders but also judges and politicians, the repositories of the knowledge of the culture's history, both sacred and secular. They are familiar with cosmic

> as well as physical geography; the ways of plants, animals, and the elements are known to them. They are psychologists, entertainers, and food finders. Above all, however, shamans are technicians of the sacred and masters of ecstasy. (Halifax, 1979, pp. 3-4)

Shamanic practices are found in many cultures ranging from Siberia (Kharitidi, 1995) to Australia (Halifax, 1979). In the United States shamans are healers within Native American communities, and shamanism has been found relevant as a spiritual practice for nonindigenous persons as well (Harner, 1982; Scott, 1992).

We offer these points for consideration:

1. For some clients, the diagnosis and treatment of mental problems may be directly linked to spiritual causes and cures.
2. For the Westernized client, alternative healing modalities from culturally diverse traditions may be effective even though the client's cultural background lacks exposure to them, presuming that the client is open, for example, to acupuncture or meditation.
3. Alternative therapies may have either explicit or implicit underpinnings of spiritual processes that aid in the healing process.
4. Alternative therapies may be complementary modalities to Western medicine and conventional counseling for clients of all cultural backgrounds (Dale, 1996).

Clearly there is a connection between spiritual beliefs and healing in the traditional cultures of the world, and it is currently emerging within Western psychology and medical practices. It is important to examine spirituality within the cultural context of clients and their developmental stages in life. We do not expect counselors to become experts in all cultural traditions, but propose that counselors must understand their own cultural framework more clearly. We suggest that they also be able to transcend cultural boundaries in order to see the commonalties of the human condition. In this way, counselors can begin to identify their own areas of competency in spiritual and multicultural issues (Fukuyama, 1990; Fukuyama & Sevig, 1997).

In Western secular society, mental health professionals might be thought to have taken on the roles of priests, shamans, and ministers. However, we do not purport to compete with spiritual leaders, or to take over these functions. It is important for mental health professionals to recognize the spiritual dimension in healing and to integrate the spiritual and psychological realms. By doing so, counselors can begin to address the important spiritual dimensions in counseling, make appropriate referrals when necessary, and work cooperatively with other healers (e.g., clergy, indigenous healers, alternative healers) in serving their clients.

Recent counseling literature seems to segment multiculturalism and spirituality. The opportunity for integration seems to be missed when only one area is examined at the expense of the other. Our experiences have shown us that people are struggling with the dilemma of understanding the meaning of diversity and multiculturalism. Mental health professionals, with their knowledge of group dynamics, attitude change, and student development and their expertise in helping people work through emotional reactions, can play an important role in multicultural conflict intervention. We believe that spiritual processes can facilitate multicultural understanding. Concurrently, the multicultural learning experience can serve as a stimulus for spiritual growth. This growth affects us as individuals, members of certain cultural groups, and as practitioners. These processes will be elaborated further in Chapter 4.

It is important to note that growth in this area is a developmental process and one in which people never fully attain being truly "multicultural" or spiritually enlightened. Learning to be multiculturally proficient is a process filled with "unlearning" and "relearning" ways people have been socialized to think of self, of others, and of the world. The tasks involved in unlearning this socialization, truly valuing difference, confronting internalized oppression, and building alliances with other people and groups are often difficult and painful. In the challenge of accomplishing these tasks, a process of change is encountered that includes both stumbling blocks and adventures. This process is accompanied by feelings of fear, anger, sadness, excitement, and happiness. It also involves a sense of loss of "what once was." With this process of change comes resistance similar to the resistance encountered in therapy; and most people are resistant to change. Resistance is a natural part of the process of making the transition from monoculturalism (or ethnocentrism) to multiculturalism. From a non-Western perspective, resistance is viewed as healthy and informative in making changes. This change process is similar to that which is experienced on the "spiritual journey" as well. Feelings of fear, excitement, and resistance from the ego are commonplace for the spiritual seeker. As such, growing and developing multiculturally helps people grow spiritually and vice versa. (See Box 1.4.)

Box 1.4

Self-Reflection Questions

Cultural Beliefs About Healing and Spirituality

1. To what extent does your cultural background incorporate spiritual beliefs as part of health and illness?
2. How do you view the healing process? Is it related to spirituality in anyway? If so, how?
3. What biases or stereotypes do you have about various cultural religious/spiritual belief systems?
4. To what extent do you feel comfortable engaging in an exploration of these issues as they relate to your role as counselor?
5. As you think about integrating spirituality into multicultural counseling, articulate your concerns, resistances, and questions.

Contemporary Contributions

Influences from transpersonal psychology, addiction recovery, and the holistic health movements have made important contributions toward including spirituality in counseling and will be mentioned briefly in this section. Transpersonal psychology has its origins in the 1960s in the United States during a period of social revolution and exploration of altered states of consciousness influenced by Eastern meditation practices and the use of psychedelic drugs. Cortright (1997) describes transpersonal psychology as historically emerging from humanistic and existential psychology, and currently encompassing the wisdom of the world religions toward the expansion of human consciousness and fulfillment of human potentialities.

The addiction recovery field has a strong emphasis on spirituality, especially in the twelve-step programs for alcoholism (AA), drug addiction (NA; Prezioso, 1986), Adult Children of Alcoholics (ACOA; Whitfield, 1987), and Sex and Love Addicts Anonymous (SLAA). The Twelve-step Program is based on the necessity of turning over one's will and life

Box 1.5

Self-Reflection Questions

Mind-Body-Spirit

What have been the emphases within your professional training regarding the interface of mind-body-spirit? In what ways can you extend your training to balance these three dimensions? In what ways does your professional training intersect with spirituality and multiculturalism (or not)?

to the care of God, however known or defined. Gerald May (1988) posits that we are all addicted to one thing or another, for example, work, ideas, relationships. He states that "addiction will prove to us that we are not gods" (p. 20). By recognizing one's powerlessness over addictions, one is led to trust in a "higher power" for guidance and healing. The shift is from self-mastery to "surrender" as one becomes willing to do God's will. This is a significant shift in focus from the usual stance taken in psychology, which emphasizes individual control.

Recent developments in the mind-body connection (Siegel, 1989; Simonton, Matthews-Simonton, & Creighton, 1978) and holistic approaches to health are recovering the spiritual dimension as an integral part of healing in modern medicine (Beck, Rawlings, & Williams, 1984; McHugh, 1987; Neuman, 1982; Peterson, 1987). There have been positive findings in studies of the effects of meditation and other relaxation techniques on physical conditions such as hypertension and chronic pain (Benson, 1993; Kabat-Zinn, 1993). Holistic models of wellness typically include the spiritual dimension along with such other major life themes as career and social, intellectual, emotional, and physical endeavors (Hettler, 1984). The holistic health movement has risen from contact between Western medicine and Eastern and indigenous healing practices (Das, 1987). (See Box 1.5.)

Innovative counseling programs around the country (Simpkinson & Simpkinson, 1997, 1998) are addressing the integration of mind-body-spirit in healing. Figure 1.2 presents a schema of various healing modalities that overlap among body, mind, and spirit.

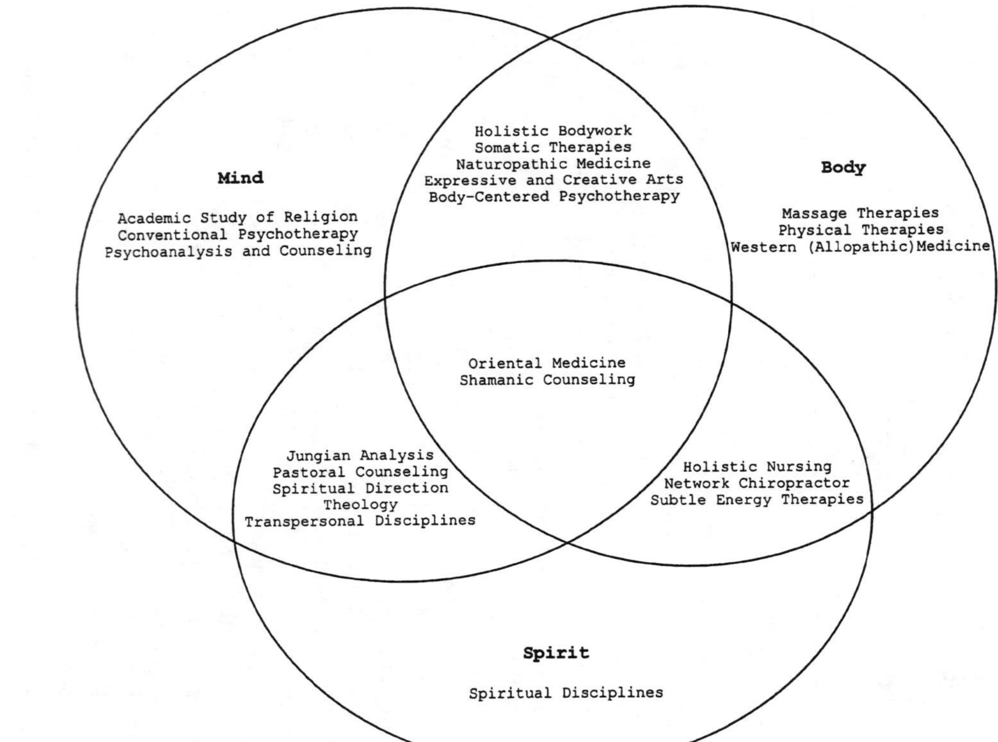

Figure 1.2. "Spectrum of Holistic Healing Modalities," adapted from *Common Boundary Graduate Education Guide* with the permission of the copyright holder, Common Boundary, Inc. 1994.

Implications for Counseling

Pedersen (1991) has suggested that multiculturalism is the "fourth force" in counseling. Cortright (1997) suggests that transpersonal psychology is the "fourth force" in psychology, building upon the psychoanalytic, behavioral, and humanistic movements. The two in combination provide an expanded view of counseling from both a content and a process perspective. We see the intersection of these forces as challenging counselors to make a paradigm shift toward understanding the human journey, which will fit more congruently with complex cultural changes facing us in the 21st century (O'Hara, 1998).

We extend an invitation to you to engage in this "journey." Just as learning the intricacies of counseling may be seen as a lifelong journey of self-exploration, growth, and service to others, so the spiritual journey invites us to deeper levels of understanding self, expanded consciousness, and service. Similarly, the multicultural journey challenges us to shift perspectives and to encompass different points of view. The process dimensions of these paths will at times overlap, run parallel, and diverge. The next chapter will focus on the spiritual journey as expressed through culture-specific worldviews.

References

Achterberg, J. (1985). *Imagery and healing. Shamanism and modern medicine.* Boston: Shambhala.

Artress, L. (1995). *Walking a sacred path: Rediscovering the labyrinth as a spiritual tool.* New York: Riverhead.

Baldwin, C. (1991). *Life's companion: Journal writing as a spiritual quest.* New York: Bantam Books.

Beck, C. M., Rawlings, R. P., & Williams, S. R. (1984). *Mental health—Psychiatric nursing. A holistic life-cycle approach.* St. Louis, MO: C. V. Mosby.

Benson, H. (1993). The relaxation response. In D. Goleman & J. Gurin (Eds.), *Mindbody medicine: How to use your mind for better health* (pp. 233-257). New York: Consumer Reports Books.

Bullis, R. K. (1996). *Spirituality in social work practice.* Washington, DC: Taylor & Francis.

Burke, M. T., & Miranti, J. G. (1995). *Counseling: The spiritual dimension.* Alexandria, VA: American Counseling Association.

Canda, E. R. (Ed.). (1998). *Spirituality in social work.* Binghamton, NY: Haworth.

Chandler, C. K., Holden, J. M., & Kolander, C. A. (1992). Counseling for spiritual wellness: Theory and practice. *Journal of Counseling & Development, 71,* 168-175.

Christensen, C. P. (1989). Cross-cultural awareness development: A conceptual model. *Counselor Education and Supervision, 28,* 270-289.

Clinebell, H. (1995). *Counseling for spiritually empowered wholeness: A hope-centered approach.* New York: Haworth Pastoral Press.

Cook, E. P., & Kelly, V. A. (1998). Spirituality and counseling. *Counseling and Human Development, 30*(6), 1-16.

Cornett, C. (1998). *The soul of psychotherapy. Recapturing the spiritual dimension in the therapeutic encounter.* New York: Free Press.

Cortright, B. (1997). *Psychotherapy and spirit: Theory and practice in transpersonal psychotherapy.* Albany: State University of New York Press.

Creedon, J. (1998, July-August). God with a million faces. *Utne Reader,* pp. 42-48.

Dale, R. A. (1996). Reconceiving hypnosis and acupuncture: Towards integration of health care modalities. *Alternative & Complementary Therapies, 2,* 405-409.

Das, A. K. (1987). Indigenous models of therapy in traditional Asian societies. *Journal of Multicultural Counseling and Development, 15,* 25-37.

Forester-Miller, H., Keel, L., & Mackie, K. (1998, March). *Spirituality in counseling: Understanding spirituality across cultures.* Workshop presentation at the American Counseling Association World Conference, Indianapolis, IN.

Fowler, J. W. (1981). *Stages of faith: The psychology of human development and the quest for meaning.* New York: Harper & Row.

Fox, M. (1976). *On becoming a musical mystical bear.* New York: Paulist Press/Deus Book.

Fukuyama, M. A. (1990). Taking a universal approach to multicultural counseling. *Counselor Education and Supervision, 30,* 6-17.

Fukuyama, M. A., & Sevig, T. D. (1997). Spiritual issues in counseling: A new course. *Counselor Education and Supervision, 36,* 233-244.

Geertz, C. (1973). *The interpretation of cultures.* New York: Basic Books.

Green, J. W. (1982). *Cultural awareness in the human services.* Englewood Cliffs, NJ: Prentice Hall.

Gonzalez-Wippler, M. (1992). *The Santeria experience.* St. Paul, MN: Llewellyn.

Halifax, J. (1979). *Shamanic voices: A survey of visionary narratives.* New York: E. P. Dutton.

Harner, M. (1982). *The way of the shaman.* New York: Bantam Books.

Hettler, W. (1984). Wellness: Encouraging a lifetime pursuit of excellence. *Health Values, 8*(4), 13-17.

Heinze, R. I. (1984). Healing in South and Southeast Asia. *PSI-Research, 3,* 136-140.

Hoge, D. (1996). Religion in America: The demographics of belief and affiliation. In E. P. Shafranske (Ed.), *Religion and the clinical practice of psychology* (pp. 21-41). Washington, DC: American Psychological Association.

Hood, R. W., Spilka, B., Hunsberger, B., & Gorsuch, R. (1996). *The psychology of religion: An empirical approach* (2nd ed.). New York: Guilford.

Ibrahim, F. A. (1985). Effective cross-cultural counseling and psychotherapy: A framework. *The Counseling Psychologist, 13,* 625-638.

Ingersoll, R. E. (1994). Spirituality, religion, and counseling: Dimensions and relationships. *Counseling and Values, 38,* 98-111.

Kabat-Zinn, J. (1993). Mindfulness meditation: Health benefits of an ancient Buddhist practice. In D. Goleman & J. Gurin (Eds.), *Mindbody medicine: How to use your mind for better health* (pp. 259-275). New York: Consumer Reports Books.

Katz, J. H. (1985). The sociopolitical nature of counseling. *The Counseling Psychologist, 13,* 615-624.

Kelly, E. W. (1995). *Spirituality and religion in counseling and psychotherapy: Diversity in theory and practice.* Alexandria, VA: American Counseling Association.

Kharitidi, O. (1995). *Entering the circle: A Russian psychiatrist's journey into Siberian shamanism.* Albuquerque, NM: Gloria Press.

Kluckhohn, F. R., & Strodtbeck, F. L. (1961). *Variations in value orientations.* Evanston, IL: Row, Peterson.

Koenig, H. G. (1997). *Is religion good for your health? The effects of religion on physical and mental health.* New York: Haworth Pastoral Press.

Krippner, S. (1984). Folk healing in Indonesia and around the world. *PSI-Research, 3*(3-4), 149-157.

Locke, D. C. (1990). A not so provincial view of multicultural counseling. *Counselor Education and Supervision, 30,* 18-25.

Maher, M. F., & Hunt, T. K. (1993). Spirituality reconsidered. *Counseling and Values, 38,* 21-28.

Maslow, A. (1971). *Farther reaches of human nature.* New York: Viking.

May, G. G. (1988). *Addiction and grace.* New York: Harper & Row.

May, R., & Yalom, I. D. (1989). Existential psychotherapy. In R. J. Corsini & D. Wedding (Eds.), *Current psychotherapies* (4th ed., pp. 363-402). Itasca, IL: F. E. Peacock.

McHugh, M. K. (Ed.). (1987). Nursing process [Special issue]. *The Wholistic Nursing Practice, 1*(3).

Myers, B. K. (1997). *Young children and spirituality.* New York: Routledge.

Myers, L. J., Speight, S. L., Highlen, P. S., Cox, C. I., Reynolds, A. L., Adams, E. M., & Hanley, C. P. (1991). Identity development and worldview: Toward an optimal conceptualization. *Journal of Counseling and Development, 70,* 54-63.

Naisbett, J., & Aburdene, P. (1990). *Megatrends 2000: Ten new directions for the 1990's.* New York: Avon Books.

Neuman, B. (1982). *The Neuman systems model: Application to nursing education and practice.* Norwalk, CT: Appleton-Century Crofts.

Nunez, L. M. (1995). *Santeria: A practical guide to Afro-Caribbean magic.* New York: Spring Publications.

O'Hara, M. (1998). Gestalt therapy as an emancipatory psychology for a transmodern world. *Gestalt Review, 2,* 154-168.

Pargament, K. I. (1997, August). *The psychology of religion and spirituality? Yes and no.* Presidential address to Division 36 at the 105th Annual Convention of the American Psychological Association, Chicago.

Pate, R. H., & Bondi, A. M. (1992). Religious beliefs and practice: An integral aspect of multicultural awareness. *Counselor Education and Supervision, 32,* 108-115.

Pedersen, P. (1988). *A handbook for developing multicultural awareness.* Alexandria, VA: American Counseling Association.

Pedersen, P. (Ed.). (1991). Multiculturalism as a fourth force in counseling [Special issue]. *Journal of Counseling and Development, 70*(1).

Pedersen, P. B. (1998). *Culture-centered counseling interventions: Striving for accuracy.* Thousand Oaks, CA: Sage.

Pedersen, P. B., Draguns, J. G., Lonner, W. J., & Trimble, J. E. (Eds.). (1996). *Counseling across cultures* (4th ed.). Thousand Oaks, CA: Sage.

Peterson, E. A. (1987). How to meet your clients' spiritual needs. *Journal of Psychosocial Nursing and Mental Health Services, 25*(5), 34-39.

Ponterotto, J. G., Casas, J. M., Suzuki, L. A., & Alexander, C. M. (Eds.). (1995). *Handbook of multicultural counseling.* Thousand Oaks, CA: Sage.

Prezioso, F. A. (1986). *Spirituality and the treatment of substance abuse.* Position paper, Michigan. (ERIC Document Reproduction Services No. ED 278 916)

Richards, P. S., & Bergin, A. E. (1997). *A spiritual strategy for counseling and psychotherapy.* Washington, DC: American Psychological Association.
Schaef, A. W. (1987). *When society becomes an addict.* New York: Harper & Row.
Scott, G. G. (1992). *Shamanism and personal mastery: Using symbols, rituals, and talismans to activate the powers within you.* New York: Paragon House.
Shafranske, E. P. (Ed.). (1996). *Religion and the clinical practice of psychology.* Washington, DC: American Psychological Association.
Shafranske, E. P., & Gorsuch, R. L. (1984). Factors associated with the perception of spirituality in psychotherapy. *Journal of Transpersonal Psychology, 16,* 231-241.
Siegel, B. (1989). *Peace, love, and healing.* New York: Harper & Row.
Simonton, O. C., Matthews-Simonton, S., & Creighton, J. L. (1978). *Getting well again.* New York: Bantam Books.
Simpkinson, A. A. (1997). Resting in God. *Common Boundary, 15*(5), 24-31.
Simpkinson, A. A., & Simpkinson, C. H. (1998). *Soul work: A field guide for spiritual seekers.* New York: HarperCollins.
Strohl, J. E. (1998). Transpersonalism: Ego meets soul. *Journal of Counseling and Development, 76,* 397-403.
Sue, D. W., Arredondo, P., & McDavis, R. J. (1992). Multicultural counseling competencies and standards: A call to the profession. *Journal of Counseling and Development, 70,* 477-486.
Sue, D. W., & Sue, D. (1990). *Counseling the culturally different: Theory and practice* (2nd ed.). New York: John Wiley.
Summit results in formation of spirituality competencies. (December, 1995). *Counseling Today,* p. 30.
Torres, E. (1984). *The folk-healer: The Mexican-American tradition of curanderismo.* Kingsville, TX: Nieves Press. (ERIC Document Reproduction Services No. ED 270 278)
Torrey, E. F. (1986). *Witch doctors and psychiatrists: The common roots of psychotherapy and its future* (Rev. ed.). New York: Harper & Row.
Vontress, C. E. (1988). An existential approach to cross-cultural counseling. *Journal of Multicultural Counseling and Development, 16,* 73-83.
Whitfield, C. L. (1987). *Healing the child within.* Deerfield Beach, FL: Health Communications.
Worthington, E. L. (1989). Religious faith across the life span: Implications for counseling and research. *The Counseling Psychologist, 17,* 555-612.
Wulff, D. M. (1997). *Psychology of religion: Classic and contemporary* (2nd ed.). New York: John Wiley.
Zúñiga, X., & Sevig, T. (1994, June). *Incorporating multiple learning goals to facilitate multicultural learning.* Presentation at the 7th Annual National Conference on Race & Ethnicity in American Higher Education, Atlanta, GA.

2

The Spiritual Journey

WORLDVIEWS

> As rivers have their source in some far off fountain, so the human spirit has its source. To find this fountain of spirit is to learn the secret of heaven and earth.
>
> —Lao-tzu, 6th century BC Chinese philosopher

Need for Conceptual Framework

In this chapter we explore the concept of the spiritual journey and the various ways in which it is viewed both psychologically and culturally. According to the Association for Spiritual, Ethical, and Religious Issues in Counseling (ASERVIC) guidelines, counselors must be able to "explain one or two models of human religious, spiritual or transpersonal development across the lifespan" ("Summit Results," 1995). We would like to recommend that counselors be able to articulate the cultural context of spiritual experiences as well.

In fact, the concept of development or growth over a life span may, in and of itself, be a culturally bound concept. The idea of growing or developing spiritually is frequently framed in psychological language, which is commonly accepted in the human services professions. The idea that people grow spiritually is a concept based on individuation and human development, which are constructs associated with Western civilization. If one looks at world cultures from an anthropological point of view, only two "mainstreams" have embraced the concepts of growth and development: far Eastern philosophies that originated in China and influenced modern Korea and Japan, and philosophies that originated in Mesopotamia and became Greco-Roman, European, and then "Western" culture. Many other cultures, including sub-Saharan African, Native American, and Australian Aboriginal, have not been oriented around the concept of growth or making spiritual progress (G. May, May 3, 1998, personal communication).

The concept of a spiritual journey denotes yet another process that in religious language is described as an "awakening" or "unfoldment" or "evolution." Psychological growth and spiritual "growth" are not equivalent but are perhaps similar and complementary processes. We propose that the two may be interactive at some level, and we will explore this more fully in Chapter 9.

This chapter will focus on spiritual journeys that are expressed through culture-specific frameworks. We will describe several different "models" of spiritual experiences that are expressed through worldviews, including: Native American spirituality (Garrett & Garrett, 1994; Matheson, 1996), Afrocentric spirituality (Frame & Williams, 1996; Nobles, 1980a), and women's spirituality (Christ, 1995a). These were selected partly due to their underrepresentation in the literature, and partly because we assume that the reader has been exposed to Judeo-Christian concepts through mainstream culture. In Chapter 3, we will focus on the spiritual journey as expressed through developmental frameworks (Fowler, 1981; Myers et al., 1991), including a discussion of the stages of mysticism (Bullis, 1996; Khan, 1988; Moody & Carroll, 1997).

Before proceeding, we will outline a conceptual framework within which to understand the universal qualities of spirituality and the commonalties that exist across all religions. This framework provides common ground for understanding a variety of multicultural expressions found both in organized religion and in diverse spiritual paths. Examples will be drawn from major world religions to illustrate these universal qualities. Clinical case examples will also be provided to demonstrate how spiritual or religious issues may be expressed in counseling.

Universal Qualities in Spirituality and Religion

We first focus on the universal qualities in the nature of spirituality that are common to all theological systems. The following concepts are taken from a "perennial philosophy" that extracts universally agreed upon concepts about the nature of spirituality from the major world religions. This conceptual framework is based on the work of Huston Smith (as cited in Cortright, 1997). The framework defines the nature of God or Higher Power from both Western and Eastern perspectives and describes different levels of identity and existence. In this section, examples will be given from the Hebrew, Christian, Islamic, Buddhist, and Hindu traditions.

How is God described or defined? From a Western perspective, God is a Personal Divine, theistic or theistic-relational in nature (e.g., Hebrew, Christian, and Islamic traditions). Cortright (1997) describes the individual as seeking a relationship with the Divine: "the soul exists in relationship to the Divine, and when it cuts itself off from the Divine, existential alienation, emptiness, or in Christian terms, 'fallenness' result" (p. 27). The goal is to "enter into deeper communion with this spiritual Power or Presence" (p. 27). The way in which this is accomplished is through spiritual practices such as love and devotion that open one to a higher power, similar to a "sacred marriage," as the soul finds fulfillment and peace.

The Hebrew tradition talks about this relationship with God as a Covenant with a chosen people. There are examples from the Hebrew scriptures that illustrate that people dialogue, argue, worship, and struggle with God. Jewish religious study models a search for truth through examining both sides of any question or issue. Contradictory views may be examined at the same time. For example: Although God, on the one hand, is so unfathomable the Name cannot be spoken, on the other hand, God is as intimate as the love between newlyweds. Box 2.1 contains a case example of religious questions being overtly expressed in counseling (fictitious names are used and details changed in all case examples to protect the anonymity of clients).

While people desire a close relationship with God, according to Judeo-Christian heritage, they also fail to follow through or they misuse their free will (The Fall, story of Adam and Eve). A loving relationship with God is seen as essential for positive self-acceptance, love, and a sense of

Box 2.1

Case Example

Rebecca, age 20, Jewish American third generation, firstborn child, comes to counseling questioning whether or not to continue at the university. She is interested in joining an Orthodox congregation, which would involve moving from Florida to the Northeast. Her parents are nonreligious Jews and have some concerns about her separating from them in such a dramatic way. How does this search for spiritual and religious meaning parallel her "separation-individuation" process, and how might she discuss this with her parents?

wholeness. To attain this relationship with God one goes through a process of confession, repentance, forgiveness, and absolution, often mediated by religious leaders. Faith becomes the foundation for self-worth. God is a source for love, wisdom, healing, and insight, and intervenes in the world through the concept of holy spirit and grace. From a Christian perspective, God's love was manifested in the life of Jesus, who calls people to loving one another responsibly. Some, but not all, forms of Christianity talk about a "personal relationship with Jesus," which illustrates this personalized approach to knowing God. Box 2.2 gives another case example in which the relational aspects of spirituality were overtly expressed in a counseling session.

Hebrew and Christian traditions have influenced the counseling field. Three key beliefs of these monotheistic worldviews are (a) the essential goodness of human beings, (b) unconditional love from the Creator, and (c) that human beings are responsible for their actions under the concept of "free will." Strong (1980) has applied these values to "Christian counseling." As mentioned, the underlying values of free will and individual responsibility are prevalent in secular psychotherapy as well. In addition, the therapeutic relationship embodies the values of unconditional love, acceptance, and genuineness.

The Protestant Reformation hastened the growth of individualism in the West. Luther preached "the supremacy of the individual conscience" (Storr, 1988, p. 79). Individualism also increased as societies became more complex, urbanized, and industrialized. The Protestant work ethic became part of the Christian ethos. Since the time of Freud, however,

Box 2.2

Case Example

Cassandra, a 21-year-old African American woman, comes to counseling because she is depressed following a breakup with her boyfriend. She had hoped that they would marry someday, and she now feels guilty for being sexually involved with him. She describes herself as being religious, but has stopped attending her (fundamentalist Christian) church because she doesn't feel worthy of God's love. She speaks about Jesus in personal language, but feels ashamed of herself and is reluctant to pray. How might a counselor discuss the intersection of relationship loss and her faith beliefs?

religion and psychology in the Western world have been separated. Freud viewed religion as regressive, and thought that seeking God was an infantile wish to return to the mother's breast (Storr, 1988). Psychologists and counselors took over the functions of ministers and priests.

Otto Rank is quoted as saying, "when religion lost the cosmos, society became neurotic. And we needed to invent psychology to deal with the neurosis" (Fox, 1983, p. 66). Without the cosmos, we are what Matthew Fox cites as an "introspective civilization" that lacks myth, mystery, or rituals. It is through introspection that one lacks connection to the cosmos with all of its diversity. Fox suggests that fall/redemption Christianity is too preoccupied with guilt, fear, law, and sin. To counteract this negative focus, Fox has focused on a creation-based spirituality.

The Islamic tradition also has its religious roots in the Middle East and shares its origins with Hebrew and Christian traditions. Muslims believe that the Prophet Muhammad is the last messenger of God, but other prophets like Abraham, Moses, and Jesus are recognized as important historical figures and messengers of God also. Central beliefs include the unity of God and all things, the recognition of Muhammed as prophet, the innate goodness of human beings, the importance of a community of faith, and the importance of living a devout and righteous life to achieve peace and harmony (Altareb, 1996). Spiritual practices include daily prayers, living in a faith community, giving to charity, fasting as a spiritual discipline, and making a pilgrimage to Mecca. At times, following the Islamic path may be difficult for young Muslims in the United States, as illustrated by the case example in Box 2.3.

Box 2.3

Case Example

Mohammed, age 21, is the son of Arab immigrants and the first to attend college. He enjoyed the freedom of his first years in school and partied with his peers. Now he has begun to question his lifestyle and feels some internalized impulse to return to Islamic practices. He wonders if he can successfully practice his religion while also being drawn toward an indulgent (e.g., alcohol and sex) and materialistic lifestyle. How might a counselor clarify these values choices?

Although the principles of Islam dictate that followers practice moderation and balance, the American media focus on Islamic fundamentalist extremists, which leads the American public to believe that all Muslims are extremists and dangerous. This is not the case, but negative stereotypes prevail.

In contrast, in the Eastern traditions, God is known as the Impersonal Divine, or nondual in nature. Nonduality refers to the unity or completeness of reality despite differences or polarities. For example, the Chinese principal of yin-yang suggests that within the opposite lies the "other," (night and day, male and female), and both opposites make the whole. Religions such as Buddhism, Advaita Vedanta, and Taoism emphasize the illusory nature of self and "the existence of a formless, nameless, impersonal spiritual reality which is ultimately revealed as the ground of being" (Cortright, 1997, p. 27). The goal is to merge the individual into the Impersonal Divine, and this is accomplished through spiritual practices such as meditation, karma yoga, and devotion. As the individual becomes aware of normal human conditioning and develops an observer self, a connection with the nondual nature (or unity) of reality becomes possible. In these traditions, mysticism tends to emphasize the Impersonal Divine and the inclusive or connecting dimension of spirituality; that is, there is no separation of self from the Divine: "Once you grasp the silent mind, you have that which cannot be lost" (M. S. Bhagavati, personal communication, March 15, 1998).

Buddhism originated in India and is a philosophy of enlightenment. The word *Buddha* means "awakened one." It is from the Sanskrit *budh,* which means "to fathom a depth, to penetrate to the bottom, to perceive, to know, to come to one's senses, to wake" (Campbell & Moyers, 1988, p. 96). The emphasis is upon consciousness, that is, the light within the

Box 2.4

Case Example

John, a 24-year-old White male, is doing graduate study in East Asian history and has studied Buddhism in his classes. He is struggling against his feelings of sexual attraction for men, and wants to be "beyond these feelings" from a spiritual view. He has tried to eliminate his ego so that he doesn't have to deal with developing a sexual identity. How might a counselor discuss this dilemma from a spiritual point of view?

light bulb (not the bulb, not the filaments). It is the experience of knowing oneness with the Divine source and with all beings. Through Buddhist "mindfulness" or awareness, one dissolves all illusions of separateness and gains insight into the impermanence of life. The cause of disease and suffering in the world is attachment.

The Eightfold Path is the prescription for becoming free of egocentrism and selfishness, through practices that develop intuitive wisdom, moral purity, and concentration (McGuire, 1980). These steps can be summarized by the following: right views or understanding, right purpose or aspiration, right speech, right conduct, right means of livelihood or vocation, right effort, right kind of awareness or mind control, and right concentration or meditation (Boisselier, 1994). The rational mind is seen as limiting one's self-concept and needs to be exhausted and set aside to allow for a holistic, intuitive knowing of reality. Different interpretations of Buddhism have been brought to North America through Japanese, Chinese, Korean, Vietnamese, and Tibetan teachers (Fields, 1992). There are as many variations in Buddhist practice as there are differences in Christian churches.

The healer in the Buddhist worldview would be the "spiritual master, or teacher." McGuire (1980) describes the Zen Master as a "clown, a comic midwife, and a mother hen," and says that the Zen Master assists with the spiritual delivery of the seeker (p. 593). Various techniques for developing consciousness include paradox, humor, and unorthodox behavior, to startle the disciple out of neurotic patterns of thinking. The result of realizing one's Buddha nature is compassion, selfless giving, wisdom, and transcendence. The power of God resides in the realization of divinity, which exists within each person, the realization of the true Self. These ideals imply an "egolessness" that can be seductive to the individual who is trying to avoid a part of self that is unacceptable, as illustrated in Box 2.4.

Box 2.5

Self-Reflection Questions

What are your adult impressions or images of God, Ultimacy, Transcendent Power? How would you describe your "relationship" with such sources of power? Do you share your spiritual experiences in community with others, and if so, how does this affect your spiritual processes?

Both Eastern and Western religions include the personal and impersonal. What differentiates them is a matter of emphasis. Hinduism values both equally, however, and God is depicted with several faces as well as seen as a unified force. Another way of expressing this concept is to say that God is both immanent (personal and present) and transcendent (impersonal and beyond our understanding). Because counselors need to be self-aware on this subject, we suggest the exercises in Box 2.5 for personal reflection.

In addition to understanding the nature of God or Ultimacy, according to Smith's framework (Cortright, 1997) there are four levels or dimensions of human identity:

1. Body
2. Mind
3. Soul (the "final locus of individuality")
4. Spirit (the atman that is Brahman/Buddha-nature) (Cortright, 1997, p.28)

The Soul is our spiritual nature, which is unique to each person. The Soul transcends the birth/death cycle. For example, the Soul reincarnates or returns to the earthly plane, according to the Hindu tradition. Spirit refers to identification with the Divine that is eternal and transcends subject-object duality. (See Box 2.6.)

Box 2.6

Self-Reflection Questions

What do you believe in terms of the concept of Soul? How do your beliefs "make meaning" for now and in the afterlife, if that is relevant to you?

Box 2.7

Self-Reflection Questions

Belief in transcendent power(s) is sometimes a stretch for the rational, analytical mind. Where do you find yourself "stretched" in terms of belief? What would you have difficulty tolerating in other beliefs? Practice self-observation on issues that "trigger" your reactions regarding alternative realities.

Finally, Smith identified four levels or dimensions of existence:

1. The terrestrial plane is observed and measured by the five senses.
2. The intermediate plane refers to psychic, subtle energies, the domain of spirits (e.g., entities), and archetypes of the unconscious (e.g., Jung).
3. The celestial plane contains the personal Divine, theistic-relational traditions, God, and Divine beings.
4. The infinite plane is depicted by the Impersonal Divine, nothing but Oneness, Divine Unity, without form, beyond all distinctions.

This framework helps to place various spiritual phenomena. For example, disembodied spirits or spirit guides are thought to be on the intermediate plane, while angels and other Divine figures are on the celestial plane. The infinite plane is addressed through a Buddhist chant known as the "heart sutra," which beseeches the Ultimate Source. In this schema, all of the diverse ways of spiritual naming and worship have credibility. However, some descriptions are believable and others not, depending upon one's personal and group beliefs. Recognizing biases in one's beliefs in this area is an important step toward self-awareness. (See Box 2.7.)

As people cultivate a relationship with God or Higher Power or Ultimacy, they begin to identify with a loving source that is outside of self, or, in some schemas, within self. This process may help people to enjoy life's experiences more fully or to cope with reality (e.g., suffering a loss). The spiritual journey may be likened to an awakening, expanding consciousness, or "being in love" (G. May, May 8, 1998, personal communication). Sometimes suffering becomes a springboard into greater spiritual awareness and connection, although this is not always the case. However, it may be a "best case scenario" when tragedy strikes.

Religion and culture frequently influence how people define themselves and their spiritual experiences. Because there is a strong overlay of individualism and free choice in Western psychology, it is natural for mental health professionals to imagine that people will seek out their own spiritual paths based upon personal preferences and values. This is not universal, however. Some people may never question their religion of birth. Because we, as authors, are trained as psychologists and counselors (not as theologians), we tend to gravitate toward psychological approaches to spirituality and imagine it to be a developmental process also. We have found through review of the psychological literature that a person's professional lens tends to shape this discussion.

For example, Richardson (1996) has organized the various world religions and spiritual paths by Myers-Briggs Personality Type (MBTI) and has suggested that people will naturally gravitate toward expressions that match their dominant cognitive functioning, which involves sensing, intuition, feeling, and thinking. The four spiritualities that describe these paths are the "journey of unity (intuition-thinking), journey of devotion (sensing-feeling), journey of works (sensing-thinking), and journey of harmony (intuition-feeling)" (p. 18). Richardson suggests that these paths are complementary, just as in the Myers-Briggs typology the various configurations of personality types balance each other. This conceptualization is a good example of how a psychological construct system may be overlaid upon the spiritual journey. There are a variety of ways in which the spiritual journey is described, however, and not all of them are rational, linear, or developmental.

In the remainder of this chapter, we will explore spirituality as expressed through culture-specific worldviews: Native American spirituality, Afrocentric spirituality, and women's spirituality.

Native American Spirituality

In this section we will describe the essential qualities of Native American and other indigenous spiritualities that are Earth-based. While there are many variations in myths and values orientations of Native Americans, some consistent beliefs include connection with nature, cooperation, protectiveness of life, and unselfishness (Duran & Duran, 1995; Garrett & Myers, 1996). A traditional Native American belief is that all of life is sacred and that human beings have a responsibility for caring for the Earth. All aspects of life (animals, plants, minerals, natural forces) are interrelated through the spiritual dimension (Matheson, 1996).

Box 2.8

Case Example

Sarah, a counselor in a university counseling center, started working with Steve, a 19-year-old American Indian student. Steve was in his second year as an "undecided" student and was struggling with career decision making. Sarah recognized that one possible aspect of worldview for some Native American people is harmony between individualism and collectivism. She worked with Steve to help him come to his own decisions, yet always asked how his family and extended family (e.g., elders, other members from his community) from his home area would react to his decisions. She also asked if this fit with his definition of spirituality and with finding his direction in life.

The circle is considered a symbol for life's processes and represents "reality" among Native Americans. The circle also represents the cycles of life, such as birth-death and the seasons. Within this model are values of balance, harmony, and connectedness to all living things. The four compass directions (East, South, West, North) are included in rituals and are frequently referred to as the Medicine Wheel. The four compass directions also represent spirit-nature-body-mind. In addition, specific qualities are associated with each direction. There may be some variations among tribes and geographic regions, but generally the East represents new beginnings, birth, and envisioning the future; the South symbolizes innocence, trust, and a time to build a foundation; the West represents strength and courage; and the North represents wisdom. Health is related to balancing these four directions. The circle continues to move in a clockwise motion without beginning or end, and may be conceptualized as a life path (LaDue, 1994). Traumatic events throw people outside of the circle, and healing is necessary to bring them back into the circle. Growth is conceptualized as circular or cyclical. From a holistic perspective, the spiritual journey is a life journey. The community and extended family are essential aspects of this web of life. For example, individual identity may more likely be defined through family or tribal affiliation than by what one does for work (Garrett & Garrett, 1994) (see Box 2.8).

Coles (1990) describes a 10-year-old Hopi girl's worldview:

> The sky watches us and listens to us. It talks to us, and it hopes we are ready to talk back. . . . Our God is the sky, and lives wherever the sky is. Our God is the sun and the moon, too; and our God is our [the Hopi] people, if we remember to stay here [on the consecrated land]. This is where we're supposed to be, and if we leave, we lose God. (p. 25)

When spirituality is based in a geographic region, what happens to people's spirituality if they are uprooted? Such has been the tragic case of many indigenous peoples.

The culture of the Mayans of Central America has been described as an Earth-based religion. In the words of Rigoberta Menchu, "every part of our culture comes from the earth. Our religion comes from maize [corn] and bean harvests, which are so vital to our community. So even if a man goes to try and make some money, he never forgets his culture springs from the earth" (as cited in Burgos-Deblay, 1984, p. 16).

In a worldview in which all things are sacred, the spirit world is found in nature, such as in the wind, the rain, animals, birds, and more. In the Mayan tradition, a *nahual* is a representative of the Earth and acts as a double or shadow for each Mayan from childhood. These spirits are assigned according to the day and time of birth and are kept secret. When children reach the age of 10 or 12 they are told about their *nahual.* This spirit helps the youth to communicate with nature and may act as a protector.

Traditionally, the Medicine Man or Woman or shaman has performed spiritual rituals for healing according to specific tribal customs. Native healers frequently come to this status by way of their own personal trials and challenges. The spiritual path may also include physically challenging rituals, such as a vision quest, purification lodges, and sacred dances.

Native rituals function in the context of relationships within communities and with the Creator. Native rituals are intended to guide a person to a deeper level of spirituality. Some rituals are physically, emotionally, and mentally challenging, such as the Sun Dance of the Lakota Sioux. Some rituals originate in specific geographic locations. They may also originate in secret medical societies where practices are kept both sacred and private.

There is a Hopi prophecy, transmitted by oral tradition, that speaks about four lost tribes: The White people, Black people, Red people, and Yellow people who have been disbursed on the planet. Each tribe has a special strength, a unique gift. There is danger if any one tribe dominates in an extreme way. It is thought that the knowledge and strengths of each tribe need to be brought together in order for the planet to survive (A. E. Heath, personal communication, September 16, 1990).

In addition to honoring the Native ways of being in "right relationship" with the planet, it is important to recognize that as a people, Native Americans continue to be oppressed by the cultural and economic domination of the White-European system. Native Americans as a collective suffer from a 500-year history of forced colonization and genocide. Wars, geographic relocation, boarding schools, and diseases have all contributed to the decimation of Native tribes and the trauma of survivors (Duran & Duran, 1995). Within this context, the issue of "cultural appropriation," that is, the taking of Native American customs and spirituality for purposes of exploitation, is a concern. Where and when is it appropriate to participate in Native rituals, and who is qualified to lead them? By custom, spiritual services are not for sale. Native Americans, rightly so, have condemned the stealing of their spiritual practices for profit (Kasee, 1995; LaDue, 1994). At the same time, Native American spiritual traditions offer a deep and necessary healing to the Western psyche. These complex and controversial issues need to be addressed further, and the plight of the indigenous peoples of this hemisphere, most of whom live in poverty, must be recognized. (See Box 2.9.)

Afrocentric Spirituality

The worldview from Western Africa has contributed to African American cultures of today. Nobles (1980a) described the essence of African philosophy as consisting of two major themes: oneness with nature and the survival of one's people. This emphasis upon collective unity and the connection of all beings describes an existence wherein religion and life are inseparable. Existence is defined in relation to God, the environment, spirits, and rhythms and cycles of life. There is a unity of Earth's systems. Time is both past and present, but based in experience (not numerical clock time). The individual does not exist alone: "I am because we are, and because we are, therefore, I am" (p. 29). One belongs to an extended kinship system that includes people, animals, plants, objects, ancestors, and the unborn. Ancestors are considered "living dead" as long as they are remembered. People suffer and rejoice together, and share in a collective responsibility and destiny.

Nobles (1980b) applied these principles to African American psychology. He suggested that a definition of self be an "extended self" that

Box 2.9

Self-Reflection Questions

What are the implications for you if you see everything about your life as sacred? Practice viewing nature as sources of spirit. Contemplate your lifestyle in terms of impact on nature, the environment, and community. Practice this for 10 minutes a day. What do you know about the indigenous peoples in your region? What is their history, and what are current social conditions like?

Consider the following scenario: George is a 30-year-old mental health counselor who has always felt drawn to images of Native Americans. He thinks that one of his great grandmothers might have been Cherokee, but this information has been kept secret in his family. George has attended several weekend workshops on Native American spirituality and gone on a "shamanic journey." He decides to adapt a drumming technique to induce a trance-like state in counseling with his clients who are interested in finding their spirit animals. What are some ethical considerations that need to be addressed before proceeding with such a practice?

includes "self as the awareness of one's historical consciousness (collective spirituality) and the subsequent sense of 'we' or being One" (p. 105). This sense of self transcends one's physical being and finite space and time, and certainly describes a sense of spirituality.

Based upon the African worldview, the values, goals, and techniques of therapy are different from the Western psychological perspective. Torrey (1986) suggested that in Nigeria symptom removal and improved interpersonal relationships are more important issues than rational thinking or individualism. Treatment would include suggestion, group therapy, and environmental manipulation.

Torrey (1986) described a type of psychological treatment in West African cultures that focused on the need for social reintegration of individuals suffering from mental disorders: "Treatment is not merely a 'doctor-patient' relationship but a form of social reintegration through the medium of social groups like the highly specialized N'jayei Society of the Mende. African medicine therefore plays a dual role designed to maintain the continuity of society as a functioning whole" (p. 105). North Americans, who are so highly individually focused, can learn from these collective societies about the importance of community.

Box 2.10

Case Example

Ron is a 23-year-old African American, firstborn and first to go to the university. He is feeling depressed because his mother is having problems with alcohol. His father has appealed to Ron for help because he is worried that she will lose her job. Ron is starting to fail in school and has appealed to his grandmother for advice. His grandmother has helped him to stay focused, yet he feels he needs to say something to his mother but is scared to do so. This has brought up many issues for Ron in terms of wanting to become his own person apart from the family, yet wanting to maintain strong family connections. How can a counselor identify family strengths as well as help Ron with individuation concerns?

This worldview redefines "self" as extended self. It portrays community and elements of survival through collective strength. Nancy Boyd-Franklin (1989) has emphasized the importance of understanding the strengths in the African American extended family and support networks through Black churches. Black churches provide not only social support in the face of institutionalized oppression like racism (Richardson, 1991), but also therapeutic responses through worship, prayer, catharsis over suffering, and validation of life experiences (Eugune, 1995). Counselors may need to look at communities and shift definitions of "client" from the individual to groups and families. For example, Shipp (1983) recommends group therapy as a preferred treatment modality for Black Americans, based upon the African American worldview. In addition, groups to support African American women's development have been formed (Jordan, 1991).

Afrocentric psychology is now recognized as an important basis for working with African American families (Jackson, 1990). The underlying value system in this approach includes a sense of relatedness to ancestors and community, and treating the family holistically from a spiritual base. White (1984) has identified other Afro-American values, such as psychological connection and interdependence, the oral tradition, creative synthesis, and fluid time perception. These values are important in the development of programs to serve African American clients. (See Box 2.10.)

Other themes from African American spirituality concern issues of liberation and social justice (Frame & Williams, 1996; Morris & Robinson, 1996). These themes are found in music (gospel and rap) and in social movements, such as fighting for civil rights and eliminating racism. The role of the African American church has been identified as important to community, social justice, and family life. Therefore, counselors may want to tap into African American cultural and spiritual resources when working with African American clients. Frame and Williams (1996) suggest exploring the role and importance of music as a form of personal expression, helping clients to access community resources and extended family, and utilizing culturally relevant metaphors and proverbs when appropriate.

West African heritage is found in spiritual traditions other than the Christian church. Worship of gods and goddesses (*orishas*) is found in Santeria, which has its origins in the Caribbean (Gonzalez-Wippler, 1992), and in Voudou of New Orleans (Teish, 1985).

Santeria is a magico-religious system that emerged from the cultural contact and struggle of West African (Yoruba) slaves and the Spanish-speaking Roman Catholic Church in the Caribbean islands. "Slaves transformed the enforced worship of the Catholic saints into the veiled worship of their spirit ancestors" (Gonzalez-Wippler, 1992, p. x). The customs in Santeria include worship of saints, observation of feasts and holidays, rituals, and making offerings and sacrifices. It is through submission that one receives power or protection from evil, or gains an ability to see the future. Santeria has been misunderstood because of the use of animal sacrifices, but it is nevertheless a viable religious practice among Latin Americans (particularly those close to the Caribbean; Sandoval, 1977).

Voudou is another spiritual practice that has received "bad press" as a religious tradition. The word literally means "Life-Principle, Genius, and Spirit" (Teish, 1985, p. x). It is Earth-based and oriented around ancestor worship, day-to-day life rituals and magic, and honoring the gods (*orishas*). Based also on West African cosmology, Voudou has been handed down since times of slavery by an oral tradition and is rich with Southern Black folklore, stories, and rituals. It is a spiritual practice that is a "living spiritual tradition of immanence," that is, seeing spiritual energy everywhere in everyday life, such as in nature, through music, or in application of charms or rituals (Teish, 1985, p. xv). (See Box 2.11.)

Experiential Model of Women's Spirituality

In this section, we will discuss a feminist approach to women's spirituality based upon the work of Carol Christ (1995a). Women's spirituality

Box 2.11

Self-Reflection Questions

How do your spiritual sensibilities inform your understanding of social justice issues, such as racism and what to do about it? How does your spiritual community address these concerns? If not, why not? The inner journey is connected to the outer journey, one without the other is incomplete. What social justice issues are of most importance to you and how can you be "part of the solution"?

How is music related to your spirituality? Some spiritual paths include drumming, dance movement, chanting, or singing. What have been your experiences relating various musical expressions to spirituality?

Religious language is often metaphorical. Use a metaphor to describe your cultural spiritual worldview; for example, "I see the world as connected by a luminescent spider web." Discuss these issues with others.

Discuss biases, prejudices, or preconceived ideas that you have had regarding African American expressions of spirituality. How can you get accurate information about these traditions?

emphasizes personal experience, empowerment, and liberation in the context of patriarchal values. In some instances, women have pursued feminist identified theology, such as through goddess worship (Bolen, 1984; Christ, 1995b; Krull, 1995), Wicca (Starhawk, 1979; Warwick, 1995), and Jewish feminism (Breitman, 1995), but this is not the main focus of this discussion.

Carol Christ (1995a) has explored women's spiritual journeys as described through women's poetry and prose. She explains that there are four experiences common to women's spiritual quest:

- Nothingness
- Awakening
- Insight
- New Naming

Although these experiences appear as a linear, stage-like model, Christ suggests that they are more spiral than linear. These stages may be experienced simultaneously and/or nonsequentially. We will discuss these four phases in more detail below.

The experience of "nothingness" refers to emptiness or self-negation (self-hatred and victimization) or existential angst. Within a patriarchal value system (a belief that males are superior), the experience of negative female self is frequently found in mainstream culture through sexism, relationship abuse, men's violence against women (rape, assault, battering), media distortions of femininity, and much more. The mere fact of growing up female in a male-defined religion excludes women and girls from recognition, roles with power, or identification with a masculine God image (Reilly, 1995). This passage may also be similar to the "dark night of the soul" from Christian mysticism, during which time one purges oneself of conventional values in the search for a deeper union with the Divine. Although there is a fear of insanity or self-annihilation during this period of existential questioning, it can be affirmed as a natural part of the spiritual journey. Letting go of social constructions of self and reality, although frightening, is also liberating. This is also a time of questioning and clarifying meaning and values.

As a result of existential searching, women have the opportunity to experience a "ground of being" or "grounding in nature" as an experientially felt form of spirituality that is called "awakening." This may come through experience in nature or in validating women's ways of knowing and being in the world. Frequently these ways of knowing involve women's body functions, such as menstruation, childbearing, nurturing others, intuition, and other "female" sources of power. Alternatively, women may come to a spiritual awakening through identification with a social justice movement (e.g., peace movement, human rights movements) that takes them beyond themselves to a deeper level of meaning. The metaphor of "awakening" has been used to describe other mystical experiences and implies that one becomes aware of something that already exists (Khan, 1988). This process of awakening may be seen as a return to self-empowerment. This is in contrast with the notion of "giving up of self," which is seen in the concept of a surrendering of ego. Mystical experiences are a part of the awakening process, as one merges with energies outside of one's ego boundaries.

Christ (1995a) believes that women may be more attuned to mystical experiences, due to social conditioning that enables women to be receptive and sensitive to the needs of others and thereby more open to receiving or merging with "other power" sources. It is through these mystical, transcendent, or transforming experiences that one achieves new "insights," new self-awareness, new self-confidences that lead one to the authentic self.

The final stage of spiritual quest is the woman's "naming" of her experiences with her own words. In this way, women are creating a new common language for their spirituality outside of the traditionally masculine ways of defining reality. "As women begin to name the word for themselves not only will they create new life possibilities for women, they will also upset the world order that has been taken for granted for centuries" (Christ, 1995a, p. 24). This phase takes women back into the world and allows them to connect to each other through a "sisterhood" that validates the many ways in which women may experience spirituality.

As a result of this spiritual quest, women are in a unique position to challenge hierarchical and dualistic thinking (male vs. female, body vs. spirit, light vs. dark, rational vs. emotional) and to bring these polarities together toward balance and wholeness. For example, women have created worship rituals using the "circle" as a model for equality of sharing and of connectedness, in contrast with worship rituals that place an altar at the front, up and away from those gathered.

We used the Carol Christ model as a guide for a discussion with a graduate seminar class on feminist theory and therapy, and will describe the process in detail here. First, we discussed the meaning of spirituality generally. The women offered descriptions such as "a lens, to make meaning, inter-connectedness, web of life, life path, everything happens for a reason, divine order, nature, rhythm, rituals to celebrate and symbolize everyday life, the sacred, present-moment awareness, mindfulness, a larger force." A brief writing exercise was utilized to begin the discussion. Participants were asked to write for 10 minutes by completing the following sentence stem: "If God were a She." Invoking a feminine higher power immediately validated women's experiences. Participants then responded to the four phases presented by Christ, understanding that they were not necessarily linear. Women were invited to respond to the phase that made most sense to them and to write about it. Some identified with the nothingness initially, either in relation to historic events or to their current situations. One woman felt that she had had an awakening to spiritual sensibilities as a child through her relationship with her grandmother, and then lost it when her grandmother died. As each person shared some spiritual insights, others were reminded of incidents or other "aha" kinds of experiences. The most positive aspect of this model was the empowerment process by which women could validate their experiences and name and claim them through their own words, not words imposed by masculine models of spirituality (Reilly, 1995). (See Box 2.12.)

Box 2.12

Self-Reflection Questions

How have issues of gender affected opportunities for you to explore religious and spiritual experiences? What are some of the benefits of a same-gender group discussion on spirituality or religious concerns? If you have not had this opportunity, seek it out.

Conclusion

This chapter has focused on both universal and culture-specific expressions of spirituality. We feel that it is important that counselors develop an understanding and a knowledge base of religious and spiritual phenomena and language. Additional readings on world religions and spirituality are recommended. However, we do not believe that counselors need to embrace or believe in all forms of spiritual expressions, obviously. Taking a multicultural and multidimensional approach, it is important for counselors to be self-aware and aware of the client's cultural and spiritual worldview. This framework then becomes a guide for exploring or addressing spiritual issues in counseling, which will be addressed in the latter half of the book.

References

Altareb, B. Y. (1996). Islamic spirituality in America: A middle path to unity. *Counseling and Values, 41,* 29-38.

Boisselier, J. (1994). *The wisdom of the Buddha.* New York: Harry N. Abrams.

Bolen, J. S. (1984). *Goddesses in every woman: A new psychology of women.* San Francisco: Harper & Row.

Boyd-Franklin, N. (1989). *Black families in therapy: A multi systems approach.* New York: Guilford.

Breitman, B. E. (1995). Social and spiritual reconstruction of self within a feminist Jewish community. In Women's spirituality, women's lives [Special issue]. *Women and Therapy: A Feminist Quarterly, 16*(2/3), 73-82.

Bullis, R. K. (1996). *Spirituality in social work practice.* Washington, DC: Taylor & Francis.

Burgos-Deblay, E. (Ed.). (1984). *I, Rigoberta Menchu, an Indian woman in Guatemala.* New York: Verso.

Campbell, J., & Moyers, B. A. (1988). *The power of myth.* Garden City, NY: Doubleday.

Christ, C. P. (1995a). *Diving deep and surfacing: Women writers on spiritual quest* (3rd ed.). Boston: Beacon.

Christ, C. P. (1995b). *Odyssey with the Goddess: A spiritual quest in Crete.* New York: Continuum Publishing.

Coles, R. (1990). *The spiritual life of children.* Boston: Houghton Mifflin.

Cortright, B. (1997). *Psychotherapy and spirit: Theory and practice in transpersonal psychotherapy.* Albany: State University of New York Press.

Duran, E., & Duran, B. (1995). *Native American postcolonial psychology.* Albany: State University of New York Press.

Eugune, T. M. (1995). There is a balm in Gilead: Black women and the Black church as agents of a therapeutic community. In Women's spirituality, women's lives [Special issue]. *Women and Therapy: A Feminist Quarterly, 16*(2/3), 55-71.

Fields, R. (1992). *How the swans came to the lake: A narrative history of Buddhism in America.* Boston: Shambhala.

Fowler, J. (1981). *Stages of faith: The psychology of human development and the quest for meaning.* San Francisco: Harper & Row.

Fox, M. (1983). *Original blessing.* Santa Fe, NM: Bear & Company.

Frame, M. W., & Williams, C. B. (1996). Counseling African Americans: Integrating spirituality into therapy. *Counseling and Values, 41,* 16-28.

Garrett, J. T., & Garrett, M. W. (1994). The path of good medicine: Understanding and counseling Native American Indians. *Journal of Multicultural Counseling and Development, 22,* 134-144.

Garrett, M. T., & Myers, J. E. (1996). The rule of opposites: A paradigm for counseling Native Americans. *Journal of Multicultural Counseling and Development, 24,* 89-104.

Gonzalez-Wippler, M. (1992). *The Santeria experience.* St. Paul, MN: Llewellyn.

Jackson, L. E. (1990, February 23). *The application of Afrocentric theory in family therapy.* Presentation at the Seventh Annual Winter Round Table on Cross-Cultural Counseling, Teachers College, Columbia University, New York.

Jordan, J. M. (1991). Counseling African American women: "Sister-friends." In C. C. Lee & B. L. Richardson (Eds.), *Multicultural issues in counseling: New approaches to diversity* (pp. 51-63). Alexandria, VA: American Counseling Association.

Kasee, C. R. (1995). Identity, recovery, and religious imperialism: Native American women and the new age. *Women & Therapy, 16*(2/3), 83-93.

Khan, H. I. (1988). *The awakening of the human spirit.* NW Lebanon, NY: Omega Publications.

Krull, M. (1995). Women's spirituality and healing. In Women's spirituality, women's lives [Special issue]. *Women and Therapy: A Feminist Quarterly, 16*(2/3), 135-147.

LaDue, R. A. (1994). Coyote returns: Twenty sweats does not an Indian expert make. *Women & Therapy, 15*(1), 93-111.

Matheson, L. (1996). Valuing spirituality among Native American populations. *Counseling and Values, 41,* 51-58.

McGuire, F. J. (1980). Strong's Christian counseling: A Buddhist response. *Personnel and Guidance Journal, 58,* 592-595.

Morris, J. R., & Robinson, D. T. (1996). Community and Christianity in the Black church. *Counseling and Values, 41,* 59-69.

Moody, H. R., & Carroll, D. (1997). *The five stages of the soul: Charting the spiritual passages that shape our lives.* Garden City, NY: Doubleday.

Myers, L. J., Speight, S. L., Highlen, P. S., Cox, C. I., Reynolds, A. L., Adams, E. M., & Hanley, C. P. (1991). Identity development and worldview: Toward an optimal conceptualization. *Journal of Counseling and Development, 70,* 54-63.

Nobles, W. W. (1980a). African philosophy: Foundations for Black psychology. In R. L. Jones (Ed.), *Black psychology* (2nd ed., pp. 23-36). New York: Harper & Row

Nobles, W. W. (1980b). Extended self: Rethinking the so-called Negro self-concept. In R. L. Jones (Ed.), *Black psychology* (2nd ed., pp. 99-105). New York: Harper & Row.

Reilly, P. (1995). The religious wounding of women. *Creation Spirituality, 11*(1), 41-45.

Richardson, B. L. (1991). Utilizing the resources of the African American church: Strategies for counseling professionals. In C. C. Lee & B. L. Richardson (Eds.), *Multicultural issues in counseling: New approaches to diversity* (pp. 65-75). Alexandria, VA: American Association for Counseling and Development (now, American Counseling Association).

Richardson, P. T. (1996). *Four spiritualities: Expressions of self, expressions of spirit: A psychology of contemporary spiritual choice.* Palo Alto, CA: Davies-Black.

Sandoval, M. (1977). Santeria: Afrocuban concepts of disease and its treatment in Miami. *Journal of Operational Psychiatry, 8*(2), 52-63.

Shipp, P. L. (1983). Counseling Blacks: A group approach. *Personnel and Guidance Journal, 62,* 108-111.

Starhawk. (1979). *The spiral dance: A rebirth of the ancient religion of the great Goddess.* San Francisco: Harper & Row.

Storr, A. (1988). *Solitude: A return to the self.* New York: Free Press.

Strong, S. R. (1980). Christian counseling: A synthesis of psychological and Christian concepts. *Personnel and Guidance Journal, 58,* 589-592.

Summit results in formation of spirituality competencies. (December, 1995). *Counseling Today* (p. 30).

Teish, L. (1985). *Jambalaya: The natural woman's book of personal charms and practical rituals.* New York: HarperCollins.

Torrey, E. F. (1986). *Witch doctors and psychiatrists: The common roots of psychotherapy and its future* (Rev. ed.). New York: Harper & Row.

Warwick, L. L. (1995). Feminist Wicca: Paths to empowerment. In Women's spirituality, women's lives [Special issue]. *Women and Therapy: A Feminist Quarterly, 16*(2/3), 121-133.

White, J. L. (1984). *The psychology of Blacks: An Afro-American perspective.* Englewood Cliffs, NJ: Prentice Hall.

3

The Spiritual Journey

DEVELOPMENTAL MODELS

> The experience of transition, a simple movement through time, easily eludes people as they cope with complex daily requirements. Yet since nothing stays still, except as we may imagine it, we all live at the transition point between now and next. It is through this movement that people stay fresh and through it that the stories of our lives grow.
>
> — Erving Polster, *Every Person's Life Is Worth a Novel* (1987, p. 67)

In this chapter we will examine cultural spiritual worldviews that are developmental in focus. These stage models of spiritual "growth" relate to faith development (Fowler, 1981, 1987), optimal identity development (Myers, 1988; Myers et al., 1991), and stages of mystical awakening (Bullis, 1996; Khan, 1988; Moody & Carroll, 1997). Although we qualified the topic of "spiritual growth" in the previous chapter as being subject to culturally determined constructs, these models are nevertheless relevant within the mental health counseling professions, which focus on individual growth and development. Moreover, as the Polster quote above suggests, although developmental stages or states are markers for change, the spaces in between may be just as valuable and revealing.

Table 3.1 Fowler's Stages of Faith Development

Stage 0: Undifferentiated faith: infant; pre-verbal issues of love and trust vs. abandonment, deprivation.

Stage 1: Intuitive-projective faith: ages 4-7; characterized by parental religious norms and values.

Stage 2: Mythic-literal faith: ages 7-12; concrete operational thinking; child makes sense out of family religious beliefs and rules.

Stage 3: Synthetic-conventional faith: ages 12 and up; early formal operational thinking; make coherence of own religious systems in context of pluralistic society; conformist faith.

Stage 4: Individuative-reflective faith: ages 18 and up; full formal operational thinking; rational worldview, seeking religious affiliations that reflect the "self" and self-responsibility.

Stage 5: Conjunctive faith: (midlife), formal operations—dialectical; reenergizing myths, rituals; symbols; reclaiming elements of self denied or ignored in previous stages; extending love and justice beyond one's religious group.

Stage 6: Universalizing faith: (minimum age 40), formal operational—synthetic; takes universal point of view and identifies with all of humanity; willing to make sacrifices for sake of transformation of all; primary identity is in union with the transcendent.

NOTE: Adapted from K. Stokes, *Faith Is a Verb: Dynamics of Adult Faith Development,* 1996, Mystic, CT: Twenty-third Publications.

Faith Development

An often-cited model of faith development was constructed by James Fowler (1981) and was based upon other human development theories, such as the works of Erikson, Levinson, Piaget, and Kohlberg. Fowler presented a linear, stage model that progresses from "undifferentiated faith" of infants through "universalizing faith" of elders and wise ones. As a stage model the following assumptions are made:

Each stage is discreet.

The model is hierarchical.

Each stage must be completed before moving on to the next one.

Growth is cumulative.

The stages, adapted from Stokes (1996), are listed in Table 3.1.

Fowler focuses on the processes of religious affiliation and self-in-relation to God or transcendent power. The model closely follows other developmental models, which include cognitive, moral, and social development. This model fits the norms of a White, middle-class population wherein individuation-separation is expected. It normalizes the process in which young people might be expected to go through a phase of questioning (Stage 4) and rethinking childhood religious beliefs, for example. While there has been criticism of the model for being linear and hierarchical, it is representative of many people's spiritual journey.

See Table 3.2 for a self-reflective exercise called "The Unfolding Tapestry of My Life" to see where you are in your faith development process. Fill in the relevant information under each column heading and chart changes over the life span.

John Westerhoff (cited in Stokes, 1996) uses the image of a tree's rings to suggest four interconnected and expanding styles of faith: experienced faith (at the core), affiliative faith, searching faith, and owned faith. Similar to Fowler's model, the first level of faith of children is that which is experienced directly (experienced faith). The next level of faith is experienced through community through a sense of belonging (affiliative faith). Young adulthood often brings on a searching faith as one begins to individuate from the family. In this stage, one is encouraged to question and to seek answers that make sense. The outer and final ring is that of owned faith, the culmination of searching, when one can claim a faith system that works for one. As the rings of a tree include all previous growth (growing outward from a core), so these stages of faith development are inclusive of previous growth but represent an expanded faith process.

These stages are similar to an identity development theory for young adults (Rowe & Marcia, 1980) that included the following four stages of identity development.

Diffuse (never having engaged in exploration, uncommitted)

Foreclosed (commitment made without exploration, usually based on parental values)

Moratorium (in the process of exploration and not yet ready for commitment)

Achieved identity (a firm commitment made after a period of exploration and values clarification)

Since clients frequently seek counseling during times of transition, counselors are in a position to validate change, exploration, and the reestablishment of the client's relationships with religious communities and with transcendent power.

Although it is commonly assumed that *faith* is a noun that describes set beliefs, Fowler (1987) and Stokes (1996) propose that faith is a verb, a dynamic of "becoming" or awakening or realization. As such, change in one's faith is implied over the life span. One of the problems with a stage model is that one stage is inferred to be better than another, yet all are

Table 3.2 The Unfolding Tapestry of My Life

Calendar Years From Birth	*"Place"— Geographic and Socioeconomic*	*Key Relationships*	*Uses & Directions of Self*	*Marker Events (Milestones)*

NOTE: Reprinted from *Faith Development and Pastoral Care*, by James W. Fowler, copyright © 1987 Fortress Press. Used by permission of Augsburg Fortress. May not be reproduced further without permission of the publisher.

Age by Year	*Events & Conditions in Society/World*	*Centers of Value and Power*	*Images of God*	*Authorities*

Box 3.1

Case Example

Barbara, age 39, White, middle-class, comes to counseling with symptoms of despondency following the birth of her second child. While she believes she has a case of postpartum depression, she is also coping with multiple losses: her father's recent death, putting her professional career "on hold" while devoting full time to parenting responsibilities, and a loss of feelings of creativity and aliveness. She grew up in a religiously conservative home but is now unaffiliated with any church. How might this time reflect a transition in terms of faith development? What activities could help her reenergize spiritually?

valid expressions of spirituality and faith. Others may object to the hierarchical "ladder" model, or of putting people into categories. Yet as in other psychological developmental theories, this theory can provide a structure in which people can validate exploration, questioning, and movements as various tasks are addressed in each stage of life. In this way, the process of changing one's affiliations, belief systems, and experiences of faith over a lifetime are validated. (See Box 3.1.)

M. Scott Peck (1987) has identified four similar stages in the spiritual journey:

1. Chaotic-antisocial
2. Formal-institutional
3. Skeptic-individual
4. Mystic-communal

In the first stage, people are basically nonspiritual and live a self-absorbed and unprincipled life. Stage 2 provides structure to the "chaos" and a moral code by which they can order their lives. However, persons in this stage are attached to the "form" of religious expression. In Stage 3, people disengage from formal institutions to seek personal meanings, and may be atheist or agnostic. In Stage 4, people gain appreciation for a greater connectedness and unity with life. However, people are rarely in only one stage, or may bounce back and forth, for example, between the stages of skepticism and unity. Peck suggested that the stage of the therapist will influence his or her effectiveness with clients. He recommended that the

Box 3.2

Self-Reflection Questions

Make a time line of your spiritual journey and notice patterns, cycles, and shifts in perspectives. How have life developmental stages affected your journey? Where are you now? As an alternative, draw or color a picture of your spiritual journey. Share with others.

counselor be one step ahead of the client; for example, Stage 2 counselors may work well with Stage 1 clients, and so on.

Batson, Schoenrade, and Ventis (1993) disagreed with the notion of a linear and hierarchical model of spiritual development. They suggested that there are three faith systems that may be seen as options of equal merit. They call these styles of faith "Extrinsic, Intrinsic, and Quest" (p. 169). The Extrinsic style is determined more by the individual's external social environment and may be seen as a "means" for spiritual attainment. The Intrinsic style is the "ends" dimension and is determined by the individual's internal needs for certainty, security, and direction in answers to existential questions. The Quest style is the degree to which the individual is involved in an open-ended, responsive dialogue, with existential questions raised by contradictions and paradoxes of life. "One style involves orthodox adherence to traditional religious beliefs; a second involves critical analysis and believing for oneself; and a third involves a symbolic and paradoxical interpretation of religious concepts" (p. 75).

Other authors have suggested that religious commitment may be described as either "extrinsic" or "intrinsic" (Allport & Ross, 1967). An extrinsic religious orientation is utilitarian and fulfills social needs and provides external validation. An intrinsic religious orientation is an internalized process wherein the individual lives out his or her beliefs and values on a daily basis (Reid, 1995).

Others have suggested that spiritual development does not follow a linear process, but rather "moves from side to side, backward and forward, as in a dance pattern" (Harris, as cited in Ganje-Fling & McCarthy, 1996, p. 256). Approaching spiritual development from this perspective, one may view change more in terms of fluctuations rather than stages, and allow for regression or deterioration as part of "progress." In other words, spiritual awakening may actually create slippage in one's sense of self as the "false self" drops away for the "authentic self." Fear, grief, and other forms of resistance may characterize this transition. (See Box 3.2.)

Optimal Identity Development

Identity development is an area in which a multicultural-spiritual integration can be helpful. Traditional identity development literature represents a body of work aimed at understanding a person's affiliation with a particular cultural group and how this affiliation affects that person's view of self, of others, and of the environment (Phinney, 1992; Sevig, 1993; Sue & Sue, 1990). Typically, research into these theories has examined identity around such variables as race, sexual orientation, gender, and multiple cultural identities (Atkinson, Morten, & Sue, 1989; Cass, 1979; Cross, 1991; Downing & Roush, 1985; Greene, 1997; Helms, 1990; McCarn & Fassinger, 1996). More recent writings and models of identity development recognize the importance of worldviews in general and of non-Western worldviews in particular as being important to people. In these theories, there is an attempt not to "fit" Western biases of development on all people. For example, the work of Naim Akbar (1989) stresses the importance of Afrocentric worldview on African American identity development.

Another psychospiritual identity model that is grounded in Afrocentric perspectives and recognizes the importance of worldviews is the "optimal theory applied to identity development" (OTAID; Myers et al., 1991), based on the theoretical work of Linda James Myers (1988). This theory has spirituality as a central component in the latter phase of a person's journey of identity development, and as such seems germane to our discussions in this book. The OTAID model will be discussed in more detail below.

A key tenet of the OTAID model is the integration of multiple worldviews, including ones from Native American cultures, Eastern philosophies, feminist ideology, African cultures, and Western creation spirituality. A key similarity of these sources of knowledge is that the material and spiritual are inseparable and that all is seen as the manifestation of spirit (Highlen et al., 1988; Myers, 1988; Myers et al., 1991). It is important to note that the process of spirtual-material unity is viewed as universal, though it may be manifested differently based on the cultural context in which it is experienced and lived. Historical factors, cultural norms, attitudes, and more, all affect how this unity is concretely manifested, and basically influence the content or the interpretation of the transformative process of material-spiritual unity.

This comprehensive model addresses limitations of other psychological identity development models. First, the integration of many worldviews addresses the lack of incorporation of different group perspectives in the

Table 3.3 Phases of the Optimal Theory Applied to Identity Development (OTAID) Model

Phase 0, Absence of Conscious Awareness
Phase 1, Individuation
Phase 2, Dissonance
Phase 3, Immersion
Phase 4, Internalization
Phase 5, Integration
Phase 6, Transformation

NOTE: Adapted from Jecmen (1989), Myers et al. (1991), and Sevig (1993).

existing models. Second, the model focuses on universal processes independent of any historical period in terms of sociopolitical forces. Third, the model incorporates the concept of multiple identities and oppressions in its formulations.

A research effort initiated by P. S. Highlen and a group of graduate students (1986) at The Ohio State University applied optimal theory to identity development based upon the commonalities of oppression. This model was developed through an emic approach from the qualitative analysis of interviews with people from various oppressed groups. This work was extended by Myers et al. (1991), and additional empirical work was done by Jecmen (1989) and Sevig (1993). This model provides a framework of identity development that is applicable across identity groups (e.g., race, gender, sexual orientation, socioeconomic class).

As the research team investigated the phenomenon of spiritual-material unity across differing cultures, support was found for a fundamental change in a person's conceptions of reality that takes place as the person develops a deeper, more expansive sense of identity. In this manner, the OTAID model addresses identity development holistically in that the "whole" of the self is viewed as greater than the sum of its parts (Myers et al., 1991). Counselors and psychologists who work with individuation issues may find this model useful in facilitating psychological and spiritual identity processes.

Phases of the OTAID Model

The specific OTAID model phases are summarized in Table 3.3. The descriptions are based on Jecmen (1989), Myers et al. (1991), and Sevig (1993). Each phase represents a unique set of characteristics that are distinct from the rest of the phases.

The phases of identity development are similar to other racial identity theories in that there is a sequential process by which people move from an externally defined self (from socialization) to an internally identified self who reclaims previously disowned or devalued parts of self. This identity process is particularly salient for persons who have social identities that are stigmatized, such as women, racial minorities, gay and lesbian persons, disabled persons, and others. The theory is also applicable to Whites who are becoming aware of the consequences of racism on their identity development.

The six phases will be described briefly (see Myers et al., 1991, and Sevig, 1993, for elaboration). The individuation phase is characteristic of people who develop an individual identity in early childhood and who have a definition of self derived from socialization, mostly from family and the dominant culture values. If most parts of this identity are reinforced by society, people will be less likely to move beyond this phase. It is characteristic of this phase to be unaware of how society has influenced one's identity and not to question the status quo.

The dissonance phase is characteristic of people who are starting to explore parts of their identity and to ask questions about what social group membership means. Members of stigmatized social groups have consciously or unconsciously internalized sociocultural values that devalue parts of self, for example, disliking one's skin color. This is called internalized oppression. People may deny or suppress this examination in order to escape the negative, and often painful, feelings associated with the process. (See Box 3.3.)

The immersion phase is characterized by people who accept others like themselves based on social group membership. This acceptance allows people to explore and value the parts of identity that were previously viewed negatively. This phase is characterized by feelings of excitement and pride and a sense of belonging. This group identity leads to strength and security, albeit tenuous, in that they are directly tied to social group membership. Feelings of anger and distrust may be directed toward the dominant culture.

The internalization phase describes people who have successfully attached feelings of self-worth associated with the part of self that was previously viewed negatively. However, this part of identity is now viewed as only one part among many in the totality of identity. People gain increased personal security through adopting a worldview. People are more tolerant and accepting of others who do not threaten this newfound sense of self.

Box 3.3

Case Example

Karen is a 20-year-old woman of American Indian descent who was adopted at age 2 by a Mormon family in Utah. They raised her in a strictly Mormon home and believe that by doing so, they have "saved" her soul. Karen attends a large West Coast university and is meeting other American Indians her age for the first time. However, she does not feel comfortable participating in American Indian activities, such as pow-wows, because her upbringing has told her that it is morally wrong. She feels a conflict between a desire to belong ethnically and loyalty to her adopted family. Here is an example of someone entering the dissonance stage around her religious and ethnic heritage. What would be your concerns as counselor in addressing these issues, particularly as she represents a "bi-cultural" dilemma?

The integration phase describes a significant change in the way people view life and act toward others and self. They understand that the root of oppression lies in the dominant culture. This phase is characterized by a strong sense of inner security that extends to relationships with others, enabling greater authenticity, unconditional positive regard, and valuing of differences.

The final phase, transformation, is characterized by people who view self and the world through spiritual awareness instead of external situations. Self is defined as "extended self" through association with ancestors, the unborn, nature, and community. All forms of life are seen as interrelated and valued. Negative experiences are interpreted as opportunities for learning. Thus, every experience offers opportunity for enrichment.

Tenets of the OTAID Model

There are several key tenets in the OTAID model. These underlying assumptions revolve around the nature of one's worldview, the nature of self, and the role of spirituality.

First, identity development is viewed as a broadening and deepening of one's worldview (Myers et al., 1991). For example, the first part of the identity development process is marked by dependency on others' views, but that might be said to be a "false self" (Phase 1: Individuation) and gradually progresses to where one is focused on individual factors, or "authentic self," irrespective of the larger community (Phase 4: Internalization). In the latter phases, one gains a sense of the ultimate community with larger forces, including the cosmic, and seeks to understand and connect with people while transcending socioculturally reinforced differences (Phase 6: Transformation). In addition, self-identity processes are viewed as an expandable and contractible spiral (Highlen et al., 1988).

The nature of self within the OTAID model is seen as multidimensional, and self-worth is inherent in one's being. Self is seen within a holistic system designed to foster peace and harmony within and between people (Myers, 1988). (See Box 3.4.)

A third tenet of the model is the role of spirituality, which has been traditionally separated from material factors in the Western worldview (Myers et al., 1991). Spirituality is seen as an integral part of "being" and therefore an important part of the OTAID model. The model posits that the process of self-knowledge and spiritual development is one of people coming to realize the integration of themselves as spiritual and material beings. Transposed onto this process are the guiding values of love, peace, harmony, and justice into which self, others, nature, and the transcendent are placed (Myers et al., 1991). An aim of optimal theory is to transform the alienation people sense when viewing themselves within a suboptimal conceptual system (Myers, 1988). The identity development process is seen as spiritual in *content* as well as in *process*.

Sevig (1993) and Sevig, Highlen, and Adams (1999) have developed the Self Identity Inventory (SII), which attempts to measure the strength of each OTAID phase. The SII has six scales, corresponding to phases 1 through 6 of the OTAID. Upon completing the SII, a profile is produced showing relative scores. The SII is a 71-item inventory with between 10 and 15 items in each phase. Initial psychometric results have been promising (see Sevig, 1993; Sevig et al., 1998). Correlations between SII scales and external measures of construct validity (e.g., a scale based on Myers's optimal theory, a Tolerance scale, and Helms's [1990] racial identity scales) have been in the predicted direction. In short, while the inventory is relatively new, the results hold promise for a psychometrically sound multicultural identity development instrument.

For counselors working with clients who are struggling with social oppression issues such as homophobia, sexism, and racism, it is helpful to understand a client's stage of identity development and to foster growth

Box 3.4

Case Example

Darrell is a 25-year-old African American male in his first year of graduate study at a predominantly White university. He came to counseling for help because he wanted to interact more with his peers in his program, feel more confident, and address issues of racism he was currently experiencing, which were starting to affect his studies. He reported he had done a lot of "inside" work on dealing with racism at his undergraduate school, which was a historically Black college; for example, he had been active in social justice issues and had a large social network. Since coming to his graduate program, however, he has been feeling isolated and said that he "didn't connect with others." In the initial assessment, it became apparent that while Darrell had done a lot of reading and talking with others, he was really more in Phase 4, Internalization, in that he had an "academic" understanding of tolerance, acceptance of others, but had not yet fully developed the stronger sense of inner security associated with Phase 5, Integration. Therefore, his relations with others were based more on initial appearances and social group membership. Counseling proceeded to help Darrell articulate more fully what was really important to him, what "connecting" with others really meant, to understand how oppression acts to hurt all people (not just members of certain groups), and to learn how to "move beyond" external criteria. The counselor used the OTAID model as a general framework both for assessment and for "visioning" for the future. The model was shared with Darrell for the purpose of visioning a road map for how to keep progressing in terms of "identity." While there were other foci in the counseling, this became an important part of Darrell's progress and change.

"into" the next stage. This may be as simple as suggesting that the client explore social group membership (e.g., attend a rap session) or clarifying issues that are contributing to dissonance. According to the OTAID model, deepening one's cultural identity is intricately linked to spirituality. (See Box 3.5.)

Box 3.5

Self-Reflection Questions

What cultural and social group memberships have you participated in (whether by choice or fate)? Notice how your awareness or consciousness about these various identities has shifted over time. How have you negotiated multiple group identities? What is happening in the larger cultural context that affects your attitudes and participation in social groups (e.g., political movements and social change)?

The above developmental models reflect an integration of self-identity with respect to organized religion, belief systems, spirituality, and social group memberships. Stages of development or evolvement also have been recognized in the spiritual seeker, specifically with respect to identification with transcendent power (God, Ultimacy, Divine Force). These stages will be discussed in the next section.

Mystical Traditions

Mysticism has at its root "mystery" and is interwoven into many spiritual and religious traditions. In the Middle Ages there were well-known mystics from the Christian tradition, such as St. Teresa of Avila (Peers, 1972) and St. John of the Cross (Peers, 1959); Hebrew tradition, such as Moses Ben Shem Tov de Leon, Kabbalist writer (Encyclopaedia Judaica, 1997); and Sufism, such as Rumi (Barks, 1995). The mystical path includes such things as contemplative prayer, meditation, and devotion. In this section, the stages of mysticism from the Zen, Judeo-Christian, and Sufi traditions will be summarized.

In Japan, the mystical spiritual journey has been depicted in a Zen story using the analogy of the ox herder (Ingram, 1997). A sequence of Japanese paintings is famous for explaining this story, the phases of the spiritual journey. In 10 pictures, a herder is first seen as seeking, yearning for the ox, a symbol of soul or primal nature. The herder cannot find the ox. Then the seeker catches sight of the ox's tracks and begins the search throughout the hills and valleys. Finally the ox is seen fully, and is

Table 3.4 Comparison of Stages of Mysticism

Moody and Carroll (1997)	*Bullis (1996)*	*Khan (1988)*
1. The Call	1. The Awakening of the Self	1. Awareness of inner yearning
2. The Search	2. The Stage of Purgation	2. Bewilderment
3. The Struggle	3. The Stage of Illumination	3. Understanding
4. The Breakthrough	4. The Stage of Penumbra	4. Sympathy and compassion
5. The Return	5. The Stage of Union	5. Communication and connection

struggled with until it is tamed. The ox and the seeker lie down together in harmony beneath a willow tree. In the next picture both disappear, which is symbolic of ego death and breakthrough into higher realms of consciousness. In the last stages, the seeker is resurrected and returns to the world to help others find their spiritual way (Moody & Carroll, 1997).

The stages of mysticism will be compared in the following discussion and are summarized in Table 3.4. The commonalties and differences will be noted. These models are based upon a synthesis of spiritual paths including both Eastern and Western mysticism (Bullis, 1996; Moody & Carroll, 1997). Hazrat Inayat Khan's (1988) stages are from the Sufi tradition.

The stages of mysticism, which are described in Table 3.4, are similar and represent some predictable phases of spiritual evolvement. It is assumed that the stages are successive and that successful resolution of each stage impacts the next one. Moody and Carroll (1997) suggest that this form of the spiritual journey begins at midlife, at an age when people's interests in spirituality intensify. Although these stages appear to be linear and logical in their sequence, they also function as a cycle and can be repeated over and over again.

Following from Moody and Carroll's model, the first stage, The Call, is realized when a person senses a disquieting voice from within, something like, "Is this all there is?" This dissatisfaction with life's meaning leads the person into a deeper exploration of the soul and life's purpose. Similarly described by Bullis (1996) and Khan (1988), this is a time of inner yearning or spiritual awakening. This sort of awakening typically happens slowly over a long period of time, although it can happen suddenly. The second stage, The Search, involves seeking a spiritual practice that enables the person to connect internally with his or her uniquely experienced spirituality. Individuals may seek a spiritual tradition and a teacher who can be trusted for guidance. From Khan's perspective, this stage may involve reactionary feelings and confusion. Stage 3, The Struggle, may involve challenges to the ego, examining life disappointments, or confronting habit patterns that keep the person stuck in old ways. This may be viewed as a "soul's passage" and has been expressed in mythological literature as fighting dragons while searching for the "Holy Grail." Bullis suggests that this may be a time when one needs to change self-defeating or harmful behaviors (Purgation). The struggle leads the person, it is hoped, to Stage 4, The Breakthrough. This stage has been described as an expansion of consciousness or awareness that gives new meaning, new capacity for joy and peace, and new experiences of the spirit within and/or without. Bullis describes this stage of Illumination as experiencing the divine in a more immediate and intimate way. Khan describes this process as a deepening in one's capacity for understanding, empathy, and compassion through learning detachment and observation. Bullis (1996) adds a letdown stage (Penumbra) that follows a spiritual "high" and describes it as an "anticlimax following the ecstatic illuminative stage" (p. 107). It is seen as a temporary period of depression when the person returns to everyday life. Resolution of these feelings is necessary for the person to flow into the final stage. Bullis's final stage is integration or union of divine consciousness with individual consciousness. He uses the analogy of a wedding or union of the "lover with the beloved." Moody and Carroll, on the other hand, suggest that Stage 5 is The Return, and also a necessary step in completing the spiritual cycle. The individual returns to ordinary life but brings new energy, commitment, and understanding, and may possibly offer to teach or guide other seekers. This is similar to Khan's final stage of communication and connection with all beings. Khan (1988) described this level of sensitivity as follows: "Once the eyes of the heart are open, man [*sic*] begins to read every leaf of the tree as a page of the sacred book" (p. 111).

Embedded in these models of mysticism is the assumption that all people have this innate capacity for "soul awakening," but that they will vary upon when this process begins. Some children may have a natural inclination to seek and to be sensitive to others, while some elderly persons may never engage at this level of consciousness. The metaphor of sleeping and awakening, however, suggests that each person has his or her own timetable or process for engaging this level of awareness. Sometimes people awaken slowly and sometimes suddenly as a result of a jolting kind of experience. However, counselors are advised neither to impose their spiritual views nor to look for ways to "wake up" clients.

Box 3.6

Self-Reflection Questions

What, if any, experience have you had with mystical or contemplative traditions? Where do you identify yourself in terms of the process related to these various stages of mysticism? How else might you describe your spiritual journey, considering the variety of models discussed in this chapter?

Spiritual practices such as meditation, prayer, concentration, and contemplation are tools for seekers to lead them toward this spiritual awakening and union or identification with their larger Nature, Divine Guidance, God, and Ultimate Source. These spiritual traditions rely upon the guidance of teachers who can assist a seeker through the esoteric practices.

However, not everyone needs to engage on an explicitly mystical path to be "spiritual." On a pragmatic level, people need to realize their purpose in life. People may be doing preliminary tasks, which are like stepping stones toward their greater or higher purpose in life, that is, spiritual attainment. They do not necessarily need to be engaged in esoteric spiritual practices in order to be on the spiritual path, the practices are simply one aspect of the overall picture. This process is similar to the previously mentioned models of faith development and optimal identity development, which indicated a gradual broadening of identification with one's spiritual source and a concurrent deepening of one's connection with others.

Each of these three models of spiritual awakening suggests that there is a progression in spiritual deepening that is motivated by an internalized force. Spiritual growth or change encompasses a spectrum of human emotions ranging from depression to elation. Struggles, pain, loss, and resistance are ingredients in this spiritual stew. The emotional processes of these stages of spiritual awakening are similar, in fact, to stages of multicultural awareness (Hoopes, 1979) and identity development (Myers et al., 1991). Resolution of life's difficulties, when connected to a higher purpose, has the potential to lead one to enhanced qualities of life expressed as love, compassion, understanding, humor, and peacefulness. Rather than presume that this is only a linear and cumulative process, we suggest that it is a process that provides glimpses of the Divine that sustain over time. (See Box 3.6.)

Conclusions

The spiritual path may be known through explicit rules and practices, or it may be as simple as being "mindful" while washing dishes (Hanh, 1987). The psychological self, or ego that is developed in relation to society, may or may not be essential to accessing the spiritual dimension. There are various views of the ego in relation to spirit: At times it plays a devil's advocate role in the spiritual evolvement processes, for example, when an ego attachment blocks or sabotages a spiritual impulse. A clinical example of this is seen when a client has a poor self-concept, feels unworthy, and continues to deny her- or himself the opportunity to be in loving relationships with others. At other times the ego is a humble servant of a higher calling, for example, when one takes a stand at the state prison as witness against capital punishment (the death penalty). Psychologists and mental health workers frequently are engaged in strengthening the ego to meet the demands of society. A strong ego is desirable before it can be surrendered for a higher good, or, in another view, to serve a higher good. Nevertheless, people may experience spirituality regardless of their intellectual or emotional status; it is not contingent upon psychological health per se.

The spiritual process may at times be like an accordion, expanding and contracting with the breath as one continues to refine awareness, consciousness, and energies. There may be lapses in consciousness, moments of emotional regression, confusion, and joy, all in the name of "spiritual development" over the life span. Another way of viewing this process is that "we are spiritual beings on a human journey." As one awakens spiritually, one is challenged to negotiate the territory of ego and social identities. The cultural bases of individual and group identities flavor the journey.

As the United States becomes more culturally diverse, there are more interracial and intercultural couples (Wehrly, 1996) and interfaith families (Eaton, 1994) who are immersed in a multicultural process, whether conscious of it or not. For example, combinations of ethnically and religiously diverse families are more and more common, such as Jewish and non-Jewish, Chinese and Filipino, African American and Japanese American, and Protestant and Catholic. Families may be religiously bicultural and may be affected by different religious influences from several generations (Rey, 1997). Finding common ground from which to share spiritual yearnings seems desirable and essential for relational happiness, be that as couples, families, or communities. Thus, the interaction of spirituality and multiculturalism becomes a relevant and worthy target for study. This will be elaborated in the next chapter.

References

Akbar, N. (1989). Nigrescence and identity: Some limitations. *The Counseling Psychologist, 17,* 258-263.

Allport, G., & Ross, J. (1967). Personal religious orientation and prejudice. *Journal of Personality and Social Psychology, 5,* 431-433.

Atkinson, D. R., Morten, G., & Sue, D. W. (Eds.). (1989). *Counseling American minorities: A cross-cultural perspective* (3rd ed.). Dubuque, IA: William C. Brown.

Barks, C. (Trans.). (1995). *The essential Rumi. New York: HarperSanFrancisco.*

Batson, C. D., Schoenrade, P., & Ventis, W. L. (1993). *Religion and the individual.* New York: Oxford University Press.

Bullis, R. K. (1996). *Spirituality in social work practice.* Washington, DC: Taylor & Francis.

Cass, V. C. (1979). Homosexual identity formation: A theoretical model. *Journal of Homosexuality, 15,* 13-23.

Cross, W. E. (1991). *Shades of Black.* Philadelphia: Temple University Press.

Downing, N. E., & Roush, K. L. (1985). From passive acceptance to active commitment: A model of feminist identity development for women. *Counseling Psychologist, 13,* 695-709.

Eaton, S. C. (1994). Marriage between Jews and non-Jews: Counseling implications. *Journal of Multicultural Counseling and Development, 22,* 210-214.

Encyclopaedia Judaica. (1997). [CD-ROM Edition Version 1.0]. Available: Judaica Multimedia (Israel) Ltd.

Fowler, J. (1981). *Stages of faith: The psychology of human development and the quest for meaning.* San Francisco: Harper & Row.

Fowler, J. (1987). *Faith development and pastoral care.* Philadelphia: Fortress Press.

Ganje-Fling, M. A., & McCarthy, P. (1996). Impact of childhood sexual abuse on client spiritual development: Counseling implications. *Journal of Counseling and Development, 74,* 253-258.

Greene, B. (1997). Ethnic minority lesbians and gay men: Mental health and treatment issues. In B. Greene (Ed.), *Ethnic and cultural diversity among lesbians and gay men* (pp. 216-239). Thousand Oaks, CA: Sage.

Hanh, T. N. (1987). *The miracle of mindfulness: A manual on meditation* (Rev. ed.). Boston: Beacon.

Helms, J. E. (1990). *Black and White racial identity: Theory, research, and practice.* New York: Greenwood.

Highlen, P. S., Myers, L. J., Hanley, C. P., Speight, S. L., Reynolds, A. L., Adams, E. M., & Cox, C. I. (1986). *Seed grant proposal.* Columbus: Ohio State University.

Highlen, P. S., Reynolds, A. L., Adams, E. M., Hanley, C. P., Myers, L. J., Cox, C. I., & Speight, S. L. (1988, August). *Self-identity development model of oppressed people: Inclusive model for all?* Paper presented at the meeting of the American Psychological Association Convention, Atlanta, GA.

Hoopes, D. S. (1979). Intercultural communication concepts and the psychology of intercultural experience. In M. D. Pusch (Ed.), *Multicultural education: A cross cultural training approach* (pp. 10-38). LaGrange Park, IL: Intercultural Network, Inc.

Ingram, P. O. (1997). *Wrestling with the ox: A theology of religious experience.* New York: Continuum Publishing.

Jecmen, D. J. (1989). *The development of an instrument to measure identity development in females: The Female Identity Development Scale.* Unpublished master's thesis, Ohio State University, Columbus.

Khan, H. I. (1988). *The awakening of the human spirit.* NW Lebanon, NY: Omega Publications.

McCarn, S. R., & Fassinger, R. E. (1996). Revisioning sexual minority identity development formation: A new model of lesbian identity and its implications for counseling and research. *The Counseling Psychologist, 24,* 508-534.

Moody, H. R., & Carroll, D. (1997). *The five stages of the soul: Charting the spiritual passages that shape our lives.* Garden City, NY: Doubleday.

Myers, L. J. (1988). *Understanding an Afrocentric world view: Introduction to an optimal psychology.* Dubuque, IA: Kendall/Hunt.

Myers, L. J., Speight, S. L., Highlen, P. S., Cox, C. I., Reynolds, A. L., Adams, E. M., & Hanley, C. P. (1991). Identity development and worldview: Toward an optimal conceptualization. *Journal of Counseling and Development, 70,* 54-63.

Peck, M. S. (1987). *The different drum: Community-making and peace.* New York: Simon & Schuster.

Peers, E. A. (1959). St. John of the Cross. In *Dark night of the soul* (E. A. Peers, Trans.). Austin, TX: ImageBooks.

Peers, E. A. (1972). St. Teresa of Avila. In *Interior castle* (E. A. Peers, Trans.). Austin, TX: ImageBooks.

Phinney, J. S. (1992). The Multigroup Ethnic Identity Measure: A new scale for use with diverse groups. *Journal of Adolescent Research, 7,* 156-171.

Polster, E. (1987). *Every person's life is worth a novel.* New York: Norton.

Reid, A. D. (1995). *An examination of religiousness and learned resourcefulness as factors in perceived level of stress.* Unpublished manuscript, University of Florida, Gainesville.

Rey, L. D. (1997). Religion as invisible culture: Knowing about and knowing with. In P. M. Brown & J. S. Shalett (Eds.), *Cross-cultural practice with couples and families* (pp. 159-177). New York: Haworth.

Rowe, I., & Marcia, J. E. (1980). Ego identity status, formal operations, and moral development. *Journal of Youth and Adolescence, 9*(2), 87-99.

Sevig, T. D. (1993). Development and validation of the Self Identity Inventory (SII): A pancultural instrument. *Dissertation Abstracts International, 54,* 08A. (University Microfilms No. 94-01353)

Sevig, T. D., Highlen, P. M., & Adams, E. (1999). *Development and validation of the Self Identity Inventory (SII): A multicultural identity development instrument.* Manuscript submitted for publication.

Stokes, K. (1996). *Faith is a verb: Dynamics of adult faith development.* Mystic, CT: Twenty-third Publications.

Sue, D. W., & Sue, D. (1990). *Counseling the culturally different: Theory and practice* (2nd ed.). New York: John Wiley.

Wehrly, B. (1996). *Counseling interracial individuals and families.* Alexandria, VA: American Counseling Association.

4

Multiculturalism and Spirituality

> If there is a real spiritual dimension linking us, so that we are all brothers and sisters in some profound and loving way, then we have a vital basis for creating peace in the world and genuinely caring for each other's welfare. . . . We will be rich in a much more important way than in the material dimension and these riches will transform our world for the better.
>
> —Charles Tart, in *Transpersonal Psychologies* (1992)

Introductory Comments

As stated in the first chapter, there is a natural home for spirituality within the multicultural literature for counselor training and professional development (Bart, 1998; Fukuyama & Sevig, 1997). We extend this discussion to focus on certain spiritual and multicultural processes that are interactive in nature and that contribute to each other in a synergistic way. The premise of this chapter is that although spirituality and multiculturalism have been seen as separate constructs, they are highly relevant and connected to each other. We posit that spiritual values and multicultural values are closely linked and inform the respective processes of spiritual evolvement and multicultural learning. Following from this, we also believe that in order to approach being truly multicultural and truly spiritual, this integration is necessary.

Both spirituality and multiculturalism are viewed in this book as "forces in motion." As such, they are ever changing within the self, being stimulated by encounters with new people, new experiences, new awareness, and new insights as to the nature of the universe. These forces in motion can be viewed as a bank account of sorts, in which withdrawals and deposits are made on an ongoing basis, with an ever-changing "balance." To view the process as static is to miss the richness and complexity of the symbiotic relationship. Just as deposits and withdrawals are made between accounts, spirituality and multiculturalism are interactive with each other. One informs the other in a never-ending "figure eight" (the infinity symbol) that grows in depth and width (or, visually, an expanding spiral).

While the literature bases for both spirituality and multiculturalism are vast and grow every year (Ponterotto & Sabnani, 1989), recent work appears to compartmentalize both of these arenas, thus missing the potential richness and depth gained from integration. In this chapter, we will make the central point that growing and developing multiculturally helps spiritual growth, and vice versa. This growth affects human development in general, and, in particular, impacts counselors and clients as members of specific identity groups, for example, "as the son of Russian Jewish immigrants."

We refer again to a definition of *spirituality* developed by leaders of the Association for Spiritual, Ethical, and Religious Values in Counseling (ASERVIC) that reads, in part, "an innate capacity and tendency to move towards knowledge, love, meaning, hope, transcendence, connectedness and compassion. It includes one's capacity for creativity, growth and the development of a values system" ("Summit Results," 1995, p. 30). The dynamic of moving toward greater understanding both inwardly and outwardly is central to multicultural processes as well.

The chapter will be organized around the following themes: (a) spiritual and multicultural competencies, (b) becoming multiculturally competent, (c) the resulting change process, (d) why spiritual values are necessary, and (e) integration of spirituality and multiculturalism.

Spiritual and Multicultural Competencies

In this section, we will examine the interface of spiritual and multicultural counseling competencies. Spiritual competencies for counselors were developed at a summit meeting sponsored by ASERVIC. They are summarized in the following 10 points ("Summit Results," 1995). The professional counselor will be able to:

1. explain the relationship between religious, spiritual and transpersonal phenomena, including similarities between the three types of phenomena;
2. describe religious, spiritual and transpersonal beliefs and practices from the perspective of diversity;
3. engage in self-exploration of one's religious, spiritual and/or transpersonal beliefs to foster self-understanding and acceptance of one's belief system;
4. describe one's religious, spiritual and/or transpersonal belief system;
5. explain one or two models of human religious, spiritual and transpersonal development across the lifespan;
6. demonstrate empathy for understanding a variety of religious, spiritual and transpersonal communication;
7. identify limits to one's tolerance of religious, spiritual and/or transpersonal phenomena and in case of intolerance, demonstrate appropriate referral skills and generate possible referral sources;
8. assess the relevance of the religious, spiritual and/or transpersonal domains in the client's therapeutic issues;
9. be receptive to, invite and/or avoid religious, spiritual and transpersonal material in the counseling process as it befits each client's expressed preferences when it is relevant for counseling; and
10. use a client's religious, spiritual or transpersonal beliefs in the pursuit of the client's therapeutic goals as befits the client's expressed preferences, or admit inability to do so in such a way that honors the client. (p. 30)

Similarly, proposed multicultural counseling competencies have been developed and are described with three main characteristics: (a) understanding the counselor's awareness of own assumptions, values, and bias; (b) understanding the worldview of the culturally different client; and (c) developing appropriate counselor intervention strategies and techniques (Sue, Arredondo, & McDavis, 1992). Within each of these three areas counselors are challenged to examine their beliefs and attitudes, develop further knowledge, and expand their counseling skills. In this 3 × 3 matrix, nine competency areas have been delineated. Experts in this area suggest that becoming culturally skilled is an active and ongoing process "which never reaches an end point" (Sue & Sue, 1990, p. 146), and that acquiring cultural competence is a "constant learning process" (Sleek, 1998).

Box 4.1

Case Example

Rosa is a 30-year-old Latina of Cuban American background. She is hospitalized for suicidal thoughts and depression. In follow-up psychiatric care, she tells her doctor that she feels out of control of her life. Upon visiting with an elderly aunt of a friend, she is told that she is possessed by her great-grandmother who died a premature, tragic death. The client is advised to follow directions for a ritual cleansing and releasing of this disembodied spirit. The client continues in therapy and also takes antidepressant medication.

Does the client divulge this spiritual interpretation to her therapist, and if so, how should the therapist respond?

There is a complementary relationship between spiritual and multicultural competencies. The spiritual competencies specify that counselors be able to describe religious, spiritual, and transpersonal expressions from culturally diverse perspectives. The multicultural competencies reinforce the importance of counselors' understanding client worldviews, which may encompasses spirituality. Counselors are asked to examine their own spiritual heritage and beliefs as well as to be aware of their cultural backgrounds. Counselors need to be able to articulate their spiritual beliefs as well as know their limits of tolerance for differences. The same could be said of multicultural competency. Finally, counselors are asked to develop assessment and intervention skills appropriate for the client's needs in both the spiritual/religious domain and in a multicultural context. For example, a multiculturally competent counselor would be willing to respect indigenous healing practices. (See Box 4.1.)

Becoming Multiculturally Competent

In the past few years many authors have proposed multicultural competencies, similar in tone to ethical guidelines published by the American Counseling Association, the American Psychological Association, and the National Association of Social Workers. Efforts to operationalize these competencies are being introduced; for example, Arredondo et al. (1996) outlined possible ways to operationalize competencies building on the work of Sue, Arredondo, and McDavis (1992) in their guidelines for working with diverse client populations. In addition, other researchers have discussed the use of preliminary instruments to measure these competencies (e.g., Pope-Davis & Dings, 1995; Ponterotto, Rieger, Barrett, & Sparks, 1994; Sodowsky, Taffe, Gutkin, & Wise, 1994).

Multiculturalism has been defined in a number of different ways in the literature (Hoopes, 1979; Jackson & Holvino, 1987). For the purposes of this chapter, we want to highlight the following processes proposed by Zúñiga and Sevig (1994). They describe certain critical dimensions of multiculturalism as including social justice, social diversity, and certain key communication processes among people. Social justice refers to working toward justice for all people, working toward reducing the impact of all "isms," and working on an institutional level (as opposed to working on an individual or cultural level). Social diversity refers to different cultural groups being represented (i.e., social identity groups based on race, gender, sexual orientation, ethnicity, religion, ability and disability status, socioeconomic status, age, and national origin). Communication processes such as dialogue, working with conflict (as opposed to conflict resolution), alliance, and coalition building between groups of people are aimed at inclusion (therefore combating exclusion) and "hearing everyone's voice." Given this, "multiculturalism" becomes a state of being, a process, an ebb and flow of kinetic forces that is aimed at inclusivity and the valuing of people for who they are. It becomes a process by which communities recognize and address culture and power differences among various social identity groups through inclusive processes and structures (Jackson & Holvino, 1987).

Hoopes (1979) describes a multicultural learning process for a pluralistic world. The stages of consciousness raising begin at ethnocentrism ("My way is the right way") and evolve through a sensitization process of awareness, understanding, acceptance, appreciation, and selective adoption of cultural skills. Knowledge of differing worldviews has a twofold effect: First, "I have a clearer idea of who I am now, because I know who I am NOT." Second, even though we are different, we are also similar; for example, for the religious, "We worship God, even though God is called different names." In realizing these connections, a feeling of separateness is gradually lessened. A paradoxical effect of clarifying and softening cultural boundaries happens simultaneously.

Zúñiga and Sevig (1994) extended the above discussion to posit that multicultural learning therefore becomes a process by which participants are able to

- recognize the impact of social group membership on individuals, groups, and communities; that is, upon one's personal identity development as well as upon that of others
- learn about the history of "my groups" in relation to the history of "other groups"; that is, uncover the relationship between the experiences of different groups within a particular social context
- understand some of the sources of social conflict between groups (e.g., patterns of dominance and subordination, cultural differences, socialized biases, institutionalized "isms," passive and active forms of discrimination)
- address "personal," "interpersonal," and "intergroup" barriers (e.g., socialized biases, internalized oppression, guilt that immobilizes, blaming)
- colearn/dialogue with one another in a coalitional learning context
- develop multicultural competencies to interact effectively in diverse/multicultural settings
- identify actions that can challenge/alter/transform social inequities

It is important to remember people take different avenues to the aspects listed above based on personality, personal experience, and social group memberships. Therefore, a model incorporating these different learning styles and multiple paths to competency building becomes helpful for individuals to "map" growth and development. One such model comes from Bailey Jackson and others from a National Training Laboratory Training Session held January 1993 in Washington, D.C. Their model (shown in Table 4.1) is based on areas of knowledge, awareness, skills, and passion, and is similar to a model for cross-cultural counselor training based on knowledge, awareness, and skills (Pedersen, 1988). Sevig and colleagues (see Note, Table 4.1) later added "action" to this model to account for the fact that oftentimes change happens at the head and heart levels, and yet the person finds it hard to extrapolate this increased awareness and knowledge to concrete, day-to-day, behaviors and actions.

The task of multicultural learning is to work continually on the above areas and recognize that people are all at different places and have different amounts of energy in these areas. It is overwhelming and unrealistic to expect people to be high on all five areas at all times, with all issues, and with all people. Therefore, it is helpful to outline a personal assessment and to work on targeted areas. (See Box 4.2.)

Table 4.1 Framework for Multicultural Competency

PERSONAL AWARENESS (Definition: awareness of self as a member of social groups and of self in a system of oppression)

- aware of the impact of my social identity group memberships on myself
- able to verbalize and act on my awareness of how my social identity group memberships impact others
- aware of the impact of my interpersonal style on others
- aware of and able to articulate my values
- able to recognize areas in which I need to grow

KNOWLEDGE (Definition: information/knowledge)

- know multiple groups' histories and experiences in this country
- recognize the history of oppression
- recognize the importance of histories of various social groups
- know models, conceptual frameworks, and terminology

SKILLS (Definition: facilitating change in individuals, groups, and systems; managing critical incidents; strategic analysis/action)

- provide feedback in a direct manner; receive feedback in an open manner
- recognize group dynamics in a manner that includes multicultural factors
- address oppressive behavior in a manner that allows others to hear and which is based on behavioral data
- able to intervene in group situations and ask probing/educational questions

PASSION (Definition: deep personal reason for caring about/doing this work and the ability to articulate this to others)

- ability to communicate compassion and empathy
- ability to communicate/share strong feelings of anger, fear, love, excitement, guilt, sorrow, etc. when appropriate
- ability to lead with heart (in addition to head)

ACTION (Definition: ability to behave/act in a manner consistent with awareness, knowledge, skills, passion)

- can interrupt oppression
- can take proactive measures against oppression
- can identify opportunities for action

NOTE: This framework was adapted in 1997 by Todd Sevig, Ximena Zúñiga, Diana Kardia, Andrea Monroe-Fowler, and Cesar Valdez from a model by Bailey Jackson, Ed.D., and the National Training Laboratory Members' Diversity Work Conference held in January 1993 in Washington, D.C.

Box 4.2

Case Example

Marshall works in a large VA hospital in a metropolitan setting and comes into contact with many diverse people and patients throughout the day. Part of his background is that he read about many different racial groups while he was in graduate school. However, he feels lacking in actually transferring this knowledge to his behavior. He has therefore outlined an action plan for himself that includes doing more "awareness" work (self-assessment, going to events in the community, and talking with people) and "action" work, and lessening the amount of "knowledge" work (reading). He plans to do this for one year and then reevaluate his strengths and weaknesses.

The Resulting Change Process

The resulting change process becomes one of "learning, unlearning, and relearning"—one that comes with many feelings (e.g., excitement, anxiety, anger, rage, guilt, frustration, happiness, love, contentment). People begin this process with their "luggage" of personal experience. These experiences are extremely varied, so there are many different types and sizes of luggage. It works when people are willing to be understanding of self and others and try to create, nurture, and maintain this "energy." Change may be difficult to see in reality as the relationship between feelings and behavior change becomes "fuzzy" and complex. For instance, people may have the same feelings repeatedly (e.g., frustration), even though they are growing in knowledge, skills, and awareness. In effect, change becomes a deepening spiral. For example, every time Penny comes into contact with a "new" person from a group different from her, she initially becomes "scared" and "anxious." However, she consciously does personal awareness and knowledge work every time this happens, so her periods of anxiety are less intense and do not last as long as before.

Conversely, when the necessary ingredients for multicultural learning and competency building are not present, there is a situation in which people are not heard, not valued, and in which communication, at least temporarily, breaks down. This is one manifestation of oppression and injustice. Some of the components of these types of situations are in the list of "multicultural communication blockers" in Box 4.3.

Box 4.3

Multicultural Communication Blockers

- blaming (victim or perpetrator)
- feeling guilty, which immobilizes (as opposed to guilt that is part of the process of unlearning and learning)
- dominant (majority) group members struggling with group membership
- targeted (minority) group members thinking they know total experience
- telling to the exclusion of listening
- listening to the exclusion of telling
- only asking questions
- not owning "your own stuff"
- focusing only on one social group identity
- struggling to deal with other people's feelings and your own feelings
- thinking dichotomously (either/or)
- wanting answers or solutions in a hurry
- separating or isolating from other people
- lashing out
- expecting others to "teach me"
- working toward multiculturalism ONLY to help minorities
- withdrawing or exiting prematurely from a process because it is too uncomfortable

For example, in a recent workshop involving a racially diverse group of people working on changing the racial climate in their unit, participants were asked to share what they wanted to get out of the workshop. Jim, a European American, stated he was there to get as much out of the day as he could. He wanted to learn from others and said that he was going to listen for the day. Doreen, an African American woman, and Nancy, an Asian American woman, immediately interrupted Jim before he finished and started to say to the whole group that they had problems with that approach. They complained that they had gone to too many workshops like this and that they were not going to stay if this was the plan. They both said they "knew most of what they needed to know about 'racial climate' issues." Everyone looked uncomfortably at the floor. If you were the workshop leader, what would you do next?

In summary, the goal of multicultural competency is to create a multicultural community: one in which all people's voices or viewpoints are heard, valued, and sought out, and one that works toward the reduction and eventual elimination of the "isms."

Why Spiritual Values Are Necessary

Experience has shown that people struggle with the dilemmas of understanding the meaning of diversity and multiculturalism. Cultural conflicts are stressful, and a multicultural society is more likely to be dynamic, challenging, and changing. Clearly, unlearning racism, confronting internalized oppression, truly valuing difference, and taking risks to build alliances are formidable and painful tasks. Helping professionals are uniquely qualified to assist individuals as they encounter these difficult transitions. Mental health professionals have much to offer multicultural learning processes, with their expertise in helping people work through defensive reactions and their knowledge of group dynamics, attitude change, and student/adult development.

What are the spiritual qualities that assist the process of multiculturalism? The interaction of such qualities as faith, creativity, patience, humor, flexibility, and the ability to detach or let go of one's point of view (even momentarily) will assist the process of becoming multiculturally skilled. Feelings of love and compassion for humanity ("we are all connected") increase the chances of working through difficult cultural differences. A reciprocal cycle of learning can yield benefits to those seeking multicultural or spiritual competency, or both.

Further, the qualities that fulfill what it means to be multicultural and to be spiritual are similar. Goals, then, are important and transcend across spiritual traditions and across social group identities. This process, however, is different from the "cultural expression of religion and spirituality." The latter is important, yet not enough. What is needed is the integra-

Table 4.2 Comparison of Spiritual and Multicultural Values

Spiritual Values	*Multicultural Values*
Connectedness w/ others	Cultural similarities
Contact & conflict w/ reality	Cultural differences
Compassion & love	Understanding & empathy
Relationship outside of self	Movement from ethnocentrism toward cultural pluralism
Social justice	Dealing with issues of oppression, advocacy
Faith	Flexibility & patience
Grace, intimacy, creativity	Commitment & humor
Sacredness & mystery	Tolerance of ambiguity
Detachment	Observational skills
Paradox	Bicultural & multicultural skills

NOTE: From M. A. Fukuyama & T. D. Sevig, *Integrating Spirituality and Multicultural Awareness,* a workshop presented at Loyola University, Chicago, November 1992.

tion of spirituality and multiculturalism, which is more abstract, yet transformational. It is more a "state of being" or a philosophical stance that ultimately can inform and guide behavior.

The multicultural-spiritual interplay continues in a spiral fashion as one becomes multiculturally competent—in short, spiritual values can help one become multiculturally competent. A process of change is encountered that includes both stumbling blocks and exciting times. This process of change is accompanied by feelings of fear, anger, sadness, excitement, and happiness. It also involves a sense of loss of what was. With this process of change comes resistance similar to the resistance encountered in therapy. Most people, and, more generally, agencies, are resistant to change. In making the transition from monoculturalism to multiculturalism, resistance becomes a natural part of the process. Again, from a non-Western perspective, resistance is viewed as healthy and informative in making changes.

Following from this, we suggest that multicultural learning fosters spiritual evolvement, and that spiritual evolvement strengthens the multicultural learning process. For example, in Table 4.2 key "values" that are salient to spirituality or multiculturalism are listed. These values will be referred to throughout the remainder of this chapter as we discuss how their integration can come together synergistically for personal awareness, development, and increased effectiveness in counseling.

Integration of Multiculturalism and Spirituality

Table 4.2 represents some of the integral values and mind-sets that are needed in multicultural-spiritual integration. In effect, they represent some of the universal qualities of spirituality and multiculturalism that are needed independent of the particular person or culture. However, it is important to know HOW to use this in the context of a particular person's (counselor and/or client) culture. In effect, HOW to implement the integration follows certain principles of multiculturalism (e.g., understanding the influence of worldview). (See Box 4.4.)

Spiritual values such as love, compassion, and connectedness (see Table 4.2) can help people deal with oppression. Thich Nhat Hanh (1997) a Vietnamese Buddhist monk, lectured about the importance of compassion in helping people who have been targeted by prejudice and discrimination, such as gays and racial minorities. He suggested that they direct compassion toward the perpetrators. By looking through the "lens of compassionate understanding," it is easier to see that perpetrators are acting out of fear, ignorance, and projections of disowned self. People who are targets can lessen the impact of such attacks by resisting internalization of such negative images. Perpetrators really do not know those persons to whom they have ascribed negative attributes. This is similar to the Christian value of "love your enemy." However, compassion or love does not mean that one consents to the oppression, nor forgives it. It means there is a deeper understanding of the root causes of the oppression, that is, self-hatred, fear, ignorance, greed, selfishness. In this case, the spiritual quality of compassion becomes a tool for self-empowerment for persons who are oppressed by hatred, prejudice, and discrimination.

Cross-cultural experiences may also aid in one's spiritual evolution. Cultural immersion into a spiritual worldview different from that of one's childhood can free one from the residual baggage associated with past traditions. For example, counselors who has rejected their childhood religion may be more open to spiritual experiences offered through a different religion or philosophy, for example, Buddhism instead of Christianity, Hinduism instead of Judaism. The effect of experiencing a different religion or spiritual perspective may be that it becomes easier to recognize the positive points of one's religion of origin. Thus, it is possible to gain a broader understanding of one's spiritual starting place through multicultural perspectives.

Storti (1990) utilized an Eastern meditation approach to coping with cultural adaptation. First, he defined the problem; that is, cross-cultural

Box 4.4

Case Example

Alberta is an African American psychologist who started counseling with Will, a gay European American. Will came to counseling to deal with the recent death of his father. Will started talking of religious and spiritual issues such as the meaning of life and death, the afterlife, and also talked of how his faith had been a "varied" journey for him over the years. Alberta, knowing how important this issue is for most people who were raised Catholic and who are gay/lesbian/bisexual, initially spent two sessions talking with Will about his religious and spiritual journey, taking into account both the integration of Will's spirituality and his sexual orientation.

contact leads to anxiety, frustration, and confusion when others do not meet culturally conditioned expectations for behavior. He analyzed the problem further by pointing out two natural responses to cultural differences: (a) people tend to assume that others are like themselves until those assumptions are confronted through difference, and (b) people tend to withdraw when they feel uncomfortable as a result of these unmet expectations. Storti has outlined a flow chart of how these emotional reactions work in a cross-cultural encounter:

> We expect others to be like us but they aren't.
> Thus, a cultural incident occurs,
> causing a reaction (anger, fear, etc.)
> which prompts us to withdraw.
> We become aware of our reaction,
> We reflect on its cause,
> and our reaction subsides.
> We observe the situation
> which results in developing culturally appropriate expectations.
> (pp. 61-62)

In this process, the ability to detach even momentarily through self-observation allows the individual some time and space to understand the situation before becoming more reactive and judgmental. It also alleviates some of the stress and anxiety associated with uncomfortable feelings that may accompany the situation. Storti recommended that people need to have cross-cultural experiences to learn to change expectations. The only way to accommodate to the differences is through observation and an understanding of why the differences are disturbing.

Often, people want to have cultural-specific information in advance to understand cultural differences. This is a common thread in the multicultural training literature. While having some cultural-specific knowledge can be helpful, it is not sufficient to make a successful adjustment. In addition, cultural-specific knowledge is often situation specific, which is changing and dynamic. The process of learning how to observe to learn behaviors is more effective in the long run that following a list of "do's and don'ts."

One might wonder if crossing cultures is worth all of the effort described above. Storti wholeheartedly agrees that is a worthwhile endeavor. First, cross-cultural contact teaches us a lot about our own culture. Through the process, it is possible to discern between one's cultural self (conditioned) and one's personality. The cultural personality is that which is the same among all members of a specific cultural group, for example, in the United States of America a preoccupation with speed and efficiency because one has to get somewhere and do something. The individual personality is unique and stands out in one's culture. It becomes easier to change aspects of one's cultural self as a result of cross-cultural encounters. A successful adaptation also leads to goodwill and understanding of others, which is a benefit to both parties. This process of observation is useful upon returning to one's home culture as well.

In sum, the cross-cultural encounter looks like this:

- be aware of reactions
- understand the reason for these reactions; refrain from premature judgment or responses
- recognize resistance (holding onto behaviors), if there is any
- apply what is learned over repeated times

There are innumerable benefits from cross-cultural experiences. Engaging in multicultural processes challenges one's sense of "reality" and expands one's horizons. It leads one into a larger worldview and greater inclusiveness and connectedness with others. Cross-cultural immersion

Box 4.5

Case Example

Michelle, a social worker, is supervising Alice, who is a first-year practicum student. Michelle identifies herself as a feminist therapist and has worked on issues related to sexism, racism, and homophobia for many years. Alice comes from a fairly conservative religious background, and announces in her first supervision session that she can't work with gay clients due to her religious beliefs. When and how should Michelle discuss this obvious conflict of values between herself and her supervisee?

also facilitates increased self-awareness and clarification of personal and cultural identities.

Just as there is a consciousness-raising process to understand the complexities of culture, there is a process of awakening to social justice issues and oppression. Spiritual values have been an important dimension for social justice work, such as using nonviolence for civil rights and seeking political freedom (e.g., Gandhi, liberation theology, Dr. Martin Luther King, Jr.). Many religions take positions about social issues, such as taking care of the poor, the homeless, and the sick. Proponents of cultural diversity are often fighting various forms of oppression (racism, homophobia, sexism, and able-ism). Religious fundamentalists are fighting against changes in social mores and norms. There seems to be a commonality of moral rightness about these causes, whether or not one is religious.

However, many times religious causes are in opposition to one another. For example, many churches in the South were divided over the issue of civil rights for Blacks in the 1950s-1960s civil rights movement. The Black church played a key role in organizing and sustaining the civil rights movement. People risked and gave their lives for justice. White clergy were challenged by Martin Luther King, Jr., to take a stand and often failed to do so (Washington, 1986). Another contemporary example is the controversy over gay and lesbian marriage, wherein various religious leaders of churches and temples have taken differing stances. In such circumstances, the moral imperative is rarely simple or agreed upon. (See Box 4.5.)

Box 4.6

Personal Reflection Exercise

1. Reflect on how you have grown and developed multiculturally. What spiritual values from Table 4.2 have helped you in this growth? What multicultural values have helped you to grow spiritually?
2. Think of a current client you are working with. What is the client's cultural context? What is the client's spiritual belief system?
3. What action steps have you recently taken? What were the results for you (internally)? What effect did this have on others (in your community, people with whom you were working, friends or family)?

There are unfortunately many instances when people are oppressed in the name of religion. For example, anti-Semitism has its roots in the formation of the early Christian church, and Martin Luther, who started the Protestant Reformation, was an anti-Semite. It is healing work when an oppressor makes amends, such as when Whites work on eliminating racism. This process is actualized when persons with privilege become "allies" of those who are disenfranchised and work toward undoing the oppression. Taking action in these areas is inspired by the phrase, "No one is free until everyone is free." Subsequently, when religiously identified people make attempts to undo these historical wrongs by making amends, a quality of healing transpires, even if one may not have personally persecuted another. It is especially meaningful when religiously identified people make attempts to undo historical wrongs even if they did not personally persecute another. For example, Paul Sherry, the current president of the United Church of Christ (a merger of Congregational and Evangelical and Reformed Churches) formally apologized to Native Hawaiians for the exploitation they suffered at the hands of 19th-century Congregational missionaries.

In working on oppression, it is commonly discovered that everyone suffers from some form of oppression and experiences some degree of privilege, although clearly some groups have suffered more than others historically and systematically. Thus, the work is one of service to each other. (See Box 4.6.)

References

Arredondo, P., Toporek, R., Brown, S. P., Jones, J., Locke, D., Sanchez, J., & Stadler, H. (1996). Operationalization of the multicultural counseling competencies. *Journal of Multicultural Counseling and Development, 24,* 42-78.

Bart, M. (1998, December). Spirituality in counseling finding believers. *Counseling Today,* p. 1, 6.

Fukuyama, M. A., & Sevig, T. D. (1992, November). *Integrating spirituality and multicultural awareness.* Workshop presentation at Loyola University, Chicago.

Fukuyama, M. A., & Sevig, T. D. (1997). Multicultural and spiritual issues in counseling: A new course. *Counselor Education and Supervision, 36,* 233-244.

Hanh, T. N. (Speaker). (1997). *To be, to be free, to be happy. Thursday dharma talk* (Cassette Recording No. 5 A, 5B). Longmont, CO: Backcountry Productions.

Hoopes, (1979). Intercultural communication concepts and the psychology of intercultural experience. In M. D. Pusch (Ed.), *Multicultural education: A cross cultural training approach* (pp. 10-38). LaGrange Park, IL: Intercultural Network, Inc.

Jackson, B. W., & Holvino, E. L. (1987). *Multicultural organizational development.* Working paper #34, Program on Conflict Management Alternatives, Ann Arbor, Michigan.

Pedersen, P. (1988). *A handbook for developing multicultual awareness.* Alexandria, VA: American Counseling Association.

Ponterotto, J. G., & Sabnani, H. B. (1989). "Classics" in multicultural counseling: A systematic five-year content analysis. *Journal of Multicultural Counseling and Development, 17,* 1, 23-37.

Ponterotto, J. G., Rieger, B. P., Barrett, A., & Sparks, R. (1994). Assessing multicultural competence: A review of instrumentation. *Journal of Counseling and Development, 72,* 316-322.

Pope-Davis, D. B., & Dings, J. G. (1995). The assessment of multicultural counseling competencies. In J. Ponterotto, M. Casas, L. Suzuki, & C. Alexander (Eds.), *Handbook of multicultural counseling* (pp. 287-311). San Francisco: Jossey-Bass.

Sleek, S. (1998, December). Psychology's cultural competence, once "simplistic," now broadening. *APA Monitor,* pp. 1, 27.

Sodowsky, G. R., Taffe, R. C., Gutkin, T. B., & Wise, S. L. (1994). Development of the Multicultural Counseling Inventory: A self-report measure of multicultural competencies. *Journal of Counseling Psychology, 41*(2), 137-148.

Storti, C. (1990). *The art of crossing cultures.* Yarmouth, ME: Intercultural Press.

Sue, D. W., Arredondo, P., & McDavis, R. J. (1992). Multicultural counseling competencies and standards: A call to the profession. *Journal of Counseling and Development, 70,* 477-483.

Sue, D. W., & Sue, D. (1990). *Counseling the culturally different: Theory and practice* (2nd ed.). New York: John Wiley.

Summit results in formation of spirituality competencies. (1995, December). *Counseling Today,* p. 30.

Tart, C. (1992). *Transpersonal psychologies: Perspectives on the mind from seven great spiritual traditions.* New York: HarperCollins.

Washington, J. M. (Ed.). (1986). *A testament of hope: The essential writings and speeches of Martin Luther King, Jr.* New York: HarperCollins.

Zúñiga, X., & Sevig, T. (1994, June). *Incorporating multiple learning goals to facilitate multicultural learning.* Presentation at the 7th Annual National Conference on Race & Ethnicity in American Higher Education, Atlanta, GA.

5

Positive and Negative Expressions of Spirituality

> Psychology's relationship to spiritual guidance has been especially interesting and dynamic. From the time of Christ until well after the Reformation, little differentiation was made between psychological and spiritual disorders. Many forms of insanity were seen as spiritual problems, caused by demonic possession or moral deficiency. . . . Within a generation after Freud's work became known, psychotherapy was in many circles supplanting spiritual and moral guidance as the primary method of alleviating mental disorders. There ensued an age in which psychologist and psychiatrists were seen by many as a kind of "new priesthood."
>
> —May, in *Care of Mind, Care of Spirit* (1982, p. 2)

Complexity and Caveats

In this chapter we will discuss some of the complexities underlying spirituality and psychosocial constructs of health. When we add a multicultural "spin" to this discussion, yet another dimension of analysis is included. We are interested in exploring the intersection of cultural context, expressions of spirituality, and understandings of what is healthy and unhealthy human behavior.

In most cultures, spirituality is not separated from the rest of life. From a holistic perspective, people's psychological well-being is inextricably intertwined with their spiritual well-being. Culture provides beliefs and practices to sustain health. This is not the case from a Western empirical perspective. The scientific method traditionally is a reductionistic system. Thus, spirituality is discussed outside of religion, religion and science are distinct disciplines, and religion is separate from state (in principle). In recent years, psychology and Western medicine have had the power to define what is meant by "healthy."

We believe that spirituality, religion, and psychology all have qualities that may be used for positive and negative purposes: For example, psychological techniques have been used to brainwash prisoners of war. Spiritual practices and psychological growth activities have been approached in dysfunctional ways. Sometimes psychological growth is an enhancement to spiritual awareness, but this is not always the case: For example, the psychological values of rationalism and self-control might work against other ways of knowing.

Similarly, spiritual evolvement does not necessarily equate with psychological development. Cortright (1997) notes that, "Spiritual growth can lead a person to the highest levels of realization while the self remains in basic psychological conflict, and conversely, a very self-actualized person who is very effective in the business world or with interpersonal relations may have no spiritual experience or interest" (p. 80). Gerald May agrees with this irony: "The lives of the great saints of any religious tradition are, I feel, good examples of that. Many were or are crazy as loons when viewed from modern psychological frames of reference" (G. May, personal communication, May 8, 1998). Finally, it has not been unusual to observe the leaders of religion and psychology mutually criticizing each other as being irrational, crazy, escapist, filled with illusion, or the work of the devil.

With these caveats in mind, we intend to explore the following three questions: (a) What is healthy spirituality? (b) What is unhealthy spirituality? (c) What distinguishes healthy and unhealthy processes?

What Is Healthy Spirituality?

First, we explore the question "what is healthy spirituality?" by drawing on perspectives from several Western disciplines: pastoral counseling (Clinebell, 1995), mental health counseling (Ingersoll, 1994, 1998), and the psychological study of religion (Pargament, 1996). In addition, we have included one Eastern discipline, the study of yoga (Ballentine & Ajaya, 1981), for purposes of a cross-cultural comparison.

From the pastoral counseling tradition, Clinebell (1995) has defined spiritual growth as that which "aims at the enhancement of our realistic hope, our meanings, our values, our inner freedom, our faith systems, our peak experiences, and our relationship with God" (p. 19). He has suggested that there are seven areas of spiritual needs:

> the need for a viable philosophy of life,
> for creative values,
> for a relationship with a loving God,
> for developing our higher self,
> for a sense of trustful belonging in the universe,
> for renewing moments of transcendence, and
> for a caring community that nurtures spiritual growth. (p. 82)

Clinebell believed that humans are inherently spiritual beings and that the only way to fulfill this potential is through relationship with the larger spiritual reality: "Our deepest growth need is to develop our transcendent potentialities, our spiritual selves" (p. 78). From a holistic perspective, he also suggested that the spiritual dimension enhances overall personal growth, which encompasses the following seven dimensions: mind, body, spirit, relationship with others, relationship with nature, work and play life, and relationship with organizations and institutions.

From Clinebell's perspective, people could assess their religious or spiritual lives by asking whether or not participation in such activities enhanced their sense of spirituality (i.e., feeling nurtured, stimulated for growth, enhanced connections with others and nature, decreased feelings of isolation or depression). He suggested that salugenic (health promoting) religion or spirituality nurtures such growth. The outcomes of one's religious participation or spiritual practices and beliefs are the best indicators of spiritual health. For example, does participation in one's church or synagogue energize or deplete one's energy?

Ingersoll (1994) identified seven dimensions of spirituality:

1. One's conception of the divine, absolute, or force greater than one's self.
2. One's sense of meaning or what is beautiful, worthwhile.
3. One's relationship with Divinity and other beings.
4. One's tolerance or negative capability for mystery.
5. Peak and ordinary experiences engaged to enhance spirituality (may include rituals or spiritual disciplines).
6. Spirituality as play.
7. Spirituality as a systemic force that acts to integrate all the dimensions of one's life (pp. 104-105).

These seven dimensions were recently revised and expanded to 10 dimensions of spiritual wellness through a modified Delphi technique using experts across religious and spiritual traditions (Ingersoll, 1998). These 10 dimensions include the following:

1. Conception of the absolute or divine
2. Meaning
3. Connectedness
4. Mystery
5. Sense of freedom
6. Experience-ritual-practice
7. Forgiveness
8. Hope
9. Knowledge-learning
10. Present-centeredness (pp. 160-161).

These dimensions have yet to be empirically examined through the development of a new measurement, the Spiritual Wellness Inventory. However, these qualitatively derived dimensions provide a structure for evaluating one's spiritual life. Ingersoll (1998) has recommended that such an instrument be used "for individuals to assess their own spiritual state and not the spiritual states of others" (p. 164).

From the discipline of the psychological study of religion, Pargament (1996) has discussed how religious practices might be useful in promoting mental health and in coping with stress. He defined *religion* as the "search for significance in ways related to the sacred . . . the religious world wraps its search for significance in higher powers; deities; ultimacy; and the beliefs, experiences, rituals, and institutions associated with these transcendent forces" (p. 216). Religion can help in dealing with crises, loss, and death through two processes, "conservation" (i.e., preserving significance in face of threat) and "transformation" (i.e., finding new sources of significance).

There are various ways of conserving significance through religious activities. Rituals such as acts of purification (e.g., fasting, praying in a sweat lodge), confession, prayer, and meditation are examples of ways to connect the sacred with everyday life concerns. Difficult situations may be interpreted religiously to conserve meaning; for example, "it was meant to be" or "it's karmic." Religion provides a moral code, such as the Judeo-Christian Ten Commandments or the Buddhist Five Precepts. Following such moral principles helps to reduce suffering for self and for others.

Alternative religious resources provide comfort through community support groups such as meditation groups or Alcoholics Anonymous meetings.

Religion also recognizes rites of passage, which are transitional points at birth, adolescence, marriage, and death. Religion has power and serves diverse purposes (social, individual, meaning, self-esteem, and community). An example of this is seen in some Latin American communities where the town is oriented around a town square highlighted by a large Catholic church. All of the community holidays and family-related ceremonies are conducted through the auspices of the church.

Studies of how religion and spirituality help people to cope with life's difficulties have found varied correlates in dealing with stress (Gartner, 1996), coping with depression (Westgate, 1996), and physical and mental health (Koenig, 1997). Gartner's review of empirical literature on the religiously committed and measures of mental health indicated that the types of measures used affected the results. Behavioral measures were more positively correlated with mental health than paper-and-pencil attitude measures. Gartner suggested that religion might provide a social structure that prevents disorders of impulse control (e.g., antisocial behaviors), but the converse problem may occur where people are overcontrolled, which can lead to rigidity and authoritarianism.

The interplay of religion and psychology is sometimes discrete and sometimes overlapping. It has been said that psychology helps people to gain control over their lives while religion helps people deal with limits of their control in terms of "ultimate or existential concerns." To paraphrase Ram Das, a spiritual teacher, "psychology helps us to arrange the furniture in the room. Religion helps us to get out of the room" (D. Hackett, personal communication, June 10, 1990). Pargament (1996) notes that the language of the sacred includes such words as "forbearance, mystery, suffering, hope, finitude, surrender, divine purpose, redemption" (p. 232). We suggest that religion and psychology play complementary roles to each other and need not be competitive or exclusive.

Due to secularization of counseling, therapists typically do not think about the health benefits that are associated with religious practices. Richards and Bergin (1997) discuss positive associations between religiosity and mental health. In this case, the authors look at research that shows a relationship between religious beliefs and practices and dimensions of mental health. For example, a religious conversion may help an individual avoid continuing in self-destructive behaviors such as in drug or alcohol abuse.

Myers (1997) has examined the usefulness of rituals for accessing the sacred, and posited that ritual process is useful for both adults and children to experience spirituality. Ritual process theory suggests that there are four core conditions necessary for rituals: invocation of sacred space, liminality, a ritual elder, and expectation of transcendence (p. 79). Liminality means that there is a feeling or expectation that important change is about to occur. Ritual elders are defined as "stewards of the boundaries of sacred space." Functionally, rituals structure and order experience and provide for conservation and transformation.

Myers (1997) suggested that these four stages of rituals for adults parallel four core conditions necessary for a "spirituality of caring" for children; that is, a hospitable space, provision of experience, presence of caring adults, and affirming hope in a learning process that transcends present conditions (p. 63). Spiritual leaders, and similarly, teachers or counselors, help to provide "scaffolding" that supports development and facilitates change, and "as change occurs, one steps into the unknown" (p. 83).

The invocation of a ritual facilitates the transition of moving from the known to the unknown by presentation of familiar objects, words, gestures, and other symbols (e.g., communion wine and bread). Typical religious rituals include ceremonies for life transitions, such as marriage, birth, death, and coming of age. Similarly, rituals for children help order their experiences, such as rituals of coming and going, eating and sleeping, playing, toileting, greeting, and saying goodbye. "Such ritual tools serve the same invoking purpose for religions that a special blanket or toy does for a child at nap time" (Myers, 1997, p. 80).

In some cases, mental health professionals may want to encourage a client to go through a ritual as part of healing old wounds, or of marking a significant transition, like a divorce. This could be done in the context of the client's community and family, or alone.

The integration of religion and society seems to be changing in contemporary American life. Edwards (1998) sees a

> profound cultural shift from largely segregated "religious" and "secular" worlds to a more integrated world that is discovering a bridging spiritual ground. [However,] there are many dangers in this new opening, including the tendency at one end to narrow spiritual reality into a securing, rigid and exclusive fundamentalism. Then at the other end there is the tendency to broaden spiritual reality to the point that it loses all specificity, depth, and sustainability. (p. 2)

The degree to which religious or spiritual practices add to one's overall health and to the health of the larger community is a difficult question to resolve given the diversity of perspectives that are prevalent in contemporary society.

Although it is assumed that religion and spirituality, at their best, help people to feel and function better in the world, this is not necessarily a unidimensional process. Some religious leaders would say that religion exists to "comfort the distressed and distress the comfortable" (L. Reimer, personal communication, September 1, 1998). It is not unusual for inspired individuals to take issue with the status quo, to challenge "reality," and to stretch beyond their own preset notions of themselves, whether that be running a marathon for the first time or demonstrating in a march on Washington, D.C.

For a cross-cultural comparison, we have included a brief summary of the study of yoga. An Eastern discipline, yoga is considered to be a spiritual practice for the study of physical and mental control and induction of altered states of consciousness (Ballentine & Ajaya, 1981). Derived from the Hindu tradition, this introspective path is predicated on the assumption that spiritual energy (prana) flows through the body and can be released from blockages through physical postures and breath practices. The word *yoga* comes from the Sanskrit root *yuj,* which means "to yoke." This refers to connecting lower levels of consciousness to higher levels of consciousness. A yoga practice focuses on the integration of body, breath, mind, consciousness, and higher consciousness (bliss). Various forms of yoga practice include *hatha* (physical exercises), *bhakti* (devotional), *karma* (service or action), and *jnana* (philosophical). Practices are directed in such a way as to facilitate a gradual evolution of consciousness that affects one in a holistic way (relationally and intrapsychically). The ultimate goal is to integrate mind-body-spirit and to actualize "pure consciousness." A Western equivalent of this process involves moving from ego identity, to observing ego, to transpersonal consciousness, to cosmic consciousness (Ballentine & Ajaya, 1981, p. 209).

How are persons on this path assessed in terms of being "healthy" or "unhealthy"? Ballentine and Ajaya (1981) distinguish between psychosis and mysticism, and conclude that an evolved person reveals an inner peace through his or her relaxed body language. Such a person reflects clear thinking, is free from fear or anger, and shows caring for the needs of others. "The authentic mystic reflects an inner discipline—despite the fact that his [*sic*] ideas and behavior may be difficult to understand" (p. 206).

What Is Unhealthy Spirituality?

Before embarking in this direction, it is important to remember that what spiritually feeds one person may be poison to another (Kelly, 1995).

In addition, the nature of this discussion is dependent upon the lens of the viewer. For instance, a psychodynamic interpretation of unhealthy spirituality is different from a Native American view. In this section we will explore definitions of unhealthy spirituality, examine dysfunctional uses of religion, and discuss religious wounding.

There are various definitions of unhealthy spirituality. Clinebell (1995) describes pathogenic or unhealthy religion or spirituality as growth blocking, resulting from rigidity, idolatry, authoritarianism, and practices that are life constricting or that deny reality. Again, we suggest looking at the outcome of religious participation before judging it to be unhealthy. For example, religious fundamentalism (which is on the rise) may be viewed as too restrictive by some. On the other hand, it may provide the structure and security needed to create order out of chaos and confusion. We would pose a question here: Can fundamentalism exist without being authoritarian? Edwards (1998) cited an example of a woman who felt that

> her Christian fundamentalism had freed her energies for all sorts of things. She no longer had to use up so much energy worrying about what was true and what to do. For her the "heart of the matter" was revealed through a literal interpretation of scripture and a community that supported those interpretations. (p. 1)

Just as this structure may liberate her, it may oppress others (Ritter & O'Neill, 1996), or she may change beliefs over the course of her lifetime (Winell, 1993). Historically, psychology and psychiatry have viewed religiosity as pathological or dependent. Currently, there is a separate classification in the fourth edition of the *Diagnostic and Statistical Manual of Mental Disorders* ([*DSM-IV*] Code V62.89) for a religious or spiritual concern that is outside the parameters of pathology. Examples of such concerns include loss or questioning of faith, problems associated with conversion to a new faith, or questioning of spiritual values that may not necessarily be related to an organized church or religious institution (American Psychiatric Association, 1994, p. 685).

From the psychodynamic tradition, Battista (1996) has used psychodynamic language (narcissism, defenses, masochism) to describe unhealthy spirituality. He differentiated between healthy and unhealthy spirituality by asking the question, is it "true or transformative or false or defensive spirituality"? True or transformative spirituality leads people to confront inauthenticity and to accept themselves as human beings. "Spiritual life is not life beyond the body, the emotions, the mind, and people" (p. 260). The transcendent is found in the ordinary.

Battista described defensive spirituality as a way one might be inhibited from expressing one's authentic self, through a spiritual attribution. For example, one might repress anger while thinking that doing so is morally superior (which leads one to suffering and masochism). This is called a "spiritual bypass" (1996, p. 255).

Other spiritual defenses included the following:

1. Submission to others, rationalized as being loving
2. Failure to ask for nurturance, rationalized by "God is all I need"
3. Failure to deal with interpersonal or sexual needs, rationalized as ascetic practice
4. Failure to deal with interpersonal problems, rationalized as "it's all a spiritual lesson" (see Battista, 1996, p. 251).

Spiritual defenses were distinguished from spiritual offensives, which Battista referred to as "narcissistic spirituality." In such instances, a person asserts that he or she is spiritually evolved and therefore is entitled to special rights and privileges that others should recognize and support. However, spirituality is intended to accept and transform people's limited natures, not to be used as an avoidance tactic.

Dysfunctional Uses of Religion

Religion may be approached in dysfunctional ways. For example, people may strive for perfection, fail, and subsequently feel worthless or guilty. Heise and Steitz (1991) discuss fundamentalist interpretations of Biblical scriptures that reinforce negative feelings about self due to unrealistic expectations. Sometimes it is unclear which comes first: People with dysfunctional patterns may seek out religious confirmation, or religious fanatics may prey on vulnerable people who take literal interpretations in a critical, judgmental way. Regardless of the cause-and-effect debate, suffice it to say that dysfunctional approaches to religion cause undue suffering in some people.

Heise and Steitz (1991) challenge a "philosophy of spiritual perfection" because they believe it results in "poor interpersonal relationships, self-destructive patterns, a myriad of addictions, and general discontent" (p. 11). There are other ways of interpreting Biblical references to perfectionism. Although perfection has been interpreted as "being without sin," no one is sinless, so no one can achieve perfection. Another way of interpreting this passage is that perfection means wholeness or complete-

Box 5.1

Case Example

Bridget was raised in an Irish Catholic home, the oldest of six children. She fulfilled the "oldest child's" role in taking care of her siblings, and went through 12 years of parochial school. As an adult of 38, she feels guilty for not attending church, but cannot bear the thought of going back. She still has bad memories of being humiliated in school by the nuns. How might a counselor address Bridget's history as a form of "religious wounding," and how might she heal from this wounding?

ness. Such an interpretation recognizes that people are on an evolving journey, which contrasts with being judged good or bad. Perhaps the difference in interpretation lies in the contrast between a rule-bound morality and an approach that endorses "being in a process of becoming."

Counselors need to be aware that sacred writings are subject to interpretation and that those who have been theologically trained may be better able to discuss various ways of making meaning of these passages. Some mental health professionals have addressed scriptural interpretations as a part of cognitive-behavior therapy with religious clients (Kelly, 1995; Propst, 1996) or have taken a social constructionist approach (Frame, 1996). We recommend that counselors receive additional training and supervision before engaging in religious interpretation with clients. However, counselors are still in an excellent position to question religious beliefs if these are perpetuating dysfunctional or hurtful attitudes and behaviors. Counselors could explore the significance of sacred writings to the presenting issues.

Religious Wounding

Religious wounding occurs when religious structures directly hurt or restrict people's authentic selves. The degree to which people are traumatized may range from the extreme of cult membership to indirect attacks such as through media coverage of controversial religious issues, such as abortion or homosexuality. Wounding can happen on both overt and covert levels, intentionally and unintentionally. (See Box 5.1.)

Box 5.2

Case Example

Bonnie's maternal grandfather, who was a nondenominational pastor, sexually abused Bonnie from the ages of 4 through 12. Her mother did not intervene because he had abused her also when she had been a child. The family lived next to the church and was involved on a daily basis. As an adult, and after many years of therapy, Bonnie has reconciled her family history related to the sexual abuse. However, she cannot trust in anything remotely Christian in nature. She has spiritual yearnings, which are expressed through social justice issues, and is drawn toward the Divine feminine expressions of spirituality. Discuss the differences between religious language and spiritual language, and how one may heal the other.

Both family structure and community influence the degree to which children are wounded by religious structures. In the case of child abuse, the following factors affect the extent of the abuse: whether the family is punitive, whether God is portrayed as a punitive figure, the ambience of the religious community, and the degree of personal autonomy allowed a child (Judy, 1996). Such abuse is particularly hurtful if the teachings of the religious community support the unquestioned parental authority under which the abuse occurs, or if the abuse is by clergy. (See Box 5.2.)

Sexism in the church has been detrimental to women's experiences of spirituality. Reilly (1995) discussed the impact of masculine models of God and religious language that has excluded the feminine and females from full participation in the church: "As a result of our immersion in male names and images of God, we have been excluded from the Divine" (p. 41). The underlying messages through church liturgy and practice have excluded females from leadership roles, implied that women are inferior to men, suggested that females are dependent upon a male figure for salvation, and restricted women's imagination to male images and not divine female images. "A woman's inability to imagine a God who looks, bleeds, feels, thinks, and experiences life as she does is an indication of how deeply she has been injured by her religious past" (p. 44). (See Box 5.3.)

Similarly, men have been restricted from experiencing spontaneous spirituality because they have been conditioned to be always "in control"

Box 5.3

Case Example

Darlene, a 23-year-old Italian American woman, discovers feminism and can no longer tolerate exclusively masculine language in church services. She is also a devout Catholic and does not want to quit the church. What are some constructive ways for her to integrate her feminism with her spirituality and religious practice?

and not to express emotions openly. Therefore, it may be more difficult for men to engage in spiritual growth activities (Kivel, 1991). Models of God as judge and authority may be more congruent with men who have been raised to play by the rules and to seek fairness. Other gender role behaviors for boys affect male participation and experience in religion and spirituality. "We don't need to hold on to a God of Wrath which simply reflects our past models of male authority. We can participate in a reality of compassion, love, and mutual respect which steadies our lives as men and helps to strengthen our relationships and our communities" (Kivel, 1991, p. 50).

The history of slavery and race relations between Euro-Americans and African Americans in this country has also influenced the development of Black churches (Morris & Robinson, 1996). Due to segregation following the Civil War, African Americans developed their own churches and religious traditions. Some churches have incorporated Black affirmative images, such as the Shrine of the Black Madonna, which is part of the Pan African Orthodox Christian Church. Such images serve the purpose of strengthening Black people's identification with the Black experience and African heritage. Other images of Black Madonnas have been found in ancient Europe and have been connected to ancient Goddess worship (Galland, 1990). Depictions of God (and Jesus) as a White male father figure may be as unacceptable to African Americans as they are to some feminists.

Other social considerations have also been subjugated to moral judgment by organized religion, including abortion, sex, divorce, and sexual orientation. Working through a gay, lesbian, or bisexual sexual orientation may become a vehicle for spiritual growth rather than condemnation (Barret & Barzan, 1996; Fortunato, 1982). The struggle for self-worth and identity by gay, lesbian, and bisexual people is connected with their spiritual life (Ritter & O'Neill, 1989). (See Box 5.4.)

Box 5.4

Case Example

Gerald is a 28-year-old African American man who is "out" as a gay man with a select number of friends. He is religious and attends the Metropolitan Community Church (MCC), which has a predominantly gay and lesbian congregation. He has always had a strong faith and feels that it has helped him get through a difficult struggle over his sexual orientation. Now that he is starting to "come out" into the gay community, he feels strongly that he wants to claim his religious identity just as strongly as his sexual identity, even though that is not particularly popular within his circle of friends. In addition, most of his friends are White. They don't understand how he can believe in a religion that has historically persecuted gays. How would you approach sorting out these multiple cultural identities?

Currently, there is a controversy between the psychological community, which purports that it is not appropriate for therapists to try to change a client's sexual orientation, and a religious minority that suggests that sexual orientation can be changed through religious conversion. The preponderance of evidence is that conversion therapy does not work and that it does more harm than good. Both the American Psychological Association and the American Psychiatric Association have passed resolutions that condemn the practice of "reparative therapy" because it has the potential for doing harm to clients (American Psychiatric Association, 1998).

In these complex times, it is not always clear what constitutes healthy or unhealthy spirituality. This question will be explored in the next section.

What Distinguishes Between Healthy and Unhealthy Spirituality?

Distinguishing between healthy and unhealthy spirituality is a complex issue because it depends on who is labeling spirituality as "healthy" or "unhealthy." The field of psychology likes to think it has the most rigorous and true test of health. Perhaps another way to approach the question

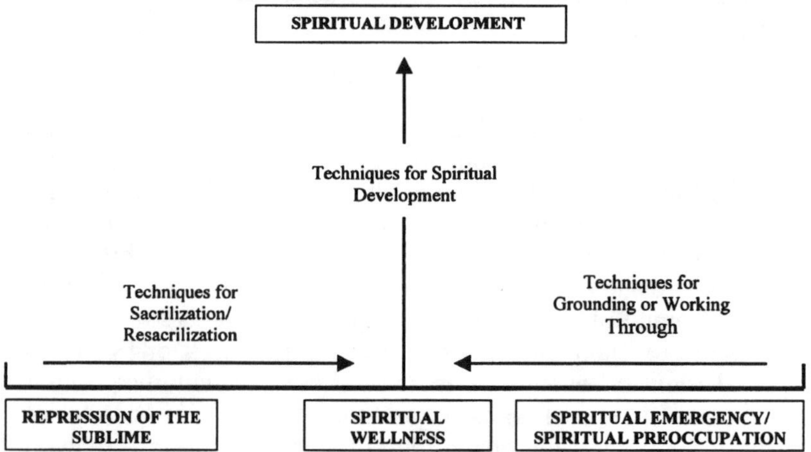

Figure 5.1. Model for Spiritual Wellness and Classes of Techniques

SOURCE: Reprinted from "Counseling for Spiritual Wellness: Theory & Practice," by Chandler, Holden, & Kolander, *Journal of Counseling & Development, 71,* p. 170. Copyright ACA. Reprinted with permission. No further reproduction authorized without written permission of the American Counseling Association.

of "what is healthy and unhealthy" is to look at various levels of functioning: internally, externally, within a family, and within a community. We suggest that psychological standards may be joined with religious and spiritual standards rather than be in opposition to one another.

Chandler, Holden, and Kolander (1992) have developed a model for spiritual wellness that has components of healthy and unhealthy spirituality; it can be seen in Figure 5.1. They define spirituality as "pertaining to the innate capacity to, and tendency to seek to, transcend one's current locus of centricity, which transcendence involves increased knowledge and love" (p. 169).

In their discussion of spiritual wellness, Chandler et al. (1992) describe a continuum from "repression of the sublime" on one end to "spiritual emergency or spiritual preoccupation" on the other end. A balance is needed between the two polarities in order to develop spiritually. For persons who have repressed their spiritual yearnings, techniques for sensitizing them to the spiritual dimension are used, such as learning meditation, prayer, visualization, dream work, or relaxation. For persons who are overly involved in spirituality or who are experiencing overwhelming energies associated with spiritual awakening, grounding exercises are more appropriate. Examples include focusing more on the physical plane, such as connecting to the Earth.

Religion can be a positive force or it can be used against people. What or who are the measures of helpfulness or hurt? What are the necessary steps for recovery from religiously based wounding?

William James (as cited in Kelly, 1995, p. 59) made the distinction between "healthy-minded" and the "sick soul" or morbid-minded individual. James suggested that when religion focuses on the negative and evil, the result is to control and limit a person's life experiences. Kelly believes that when this fear is the basis of religion, the result is "personal and social havoc."

Kelly suggests that both positive and negative effects of religion and spirituality be explored: healthy/mature versus unhealthy/immature expressions of spirituality and religion; spiritual well-being versus spiritual distress. He recommends that this be done in the assessment phase of counseling. Kelly also cites the works of Paul Pruyser, a psychodynamically oriented clinician, who described neurotic religion as being constrictive of thought and emotion. As examples, Pruyser included such defenses as disassociation, denial, displacement of conflicts, and obsessive-compulsive religiosity (Kelly, 1995, p. 64). Again, this is an example of overlaying a psychological and psychiatric language system on religious processes. It is interesting to note that Freud thought religion was an illusion, and religious leaders (e.g., Buddhist teachers) label the mind-thought process as "illusion."

Some people who are experiencing a spiritual awakening may enter into an altered state of consciousness that may appear to have psychotic features. Grof and Grof (1989) conceptualized such episodes as "spiritual emergence and emergencies" and recognized them as a normal part of the spiritual journey for some people. This type of crisis was defined as a spiritual awakening that had transformational qualities for personal growth and change. However, there has been confusion about the legitimacy and importance of these experiences due to their transpersonal nature, for example, the experiencing of nonordinary reality, mystical experiences, or unusual states of mind: "Episodes of this kind have been described in sacred literature of all ages as a result of meditative practices and as signposts of the mystical path" (Grof & Grof, 1989, p. x). The authors emphasize that it is important to distinguish between visionary states that are primarily spiritual in nature and psychosis: "While traditional approaches tend to pathologize mystical states, there is the opposite danger of spiritualizing psychotic states. . . . Transpersonal counseling is not appropriate for conditions of a clearly psychotic nature, characterized by lack of insight, paranoid delusions and hallucinations, and extravagant forms of behavior" (p. xiii).

What triggers a spiritual emergency? Sometimes traumatic events or other intense emotional experiences can trigger these experiences, such as childbirth, near death, accidents, surgery, use of psychedelic drugs, or loss, or more commonly as a result of meditative or contemplative spiritual practices (e.g., yoga, Vipassana Buddhist meditation, Christian monastic contemplation). "The experiential spectrum of spiritual emergencies is extremely rich: it involves intense emotions, visions and other changes of perception, and unusual thought processes, as well as various physical symptoms ranging from tremors to feelings of suffocation" (p. 8).

Because psychologists are steeped in Western scientific rationalism, these experiences are difficult to explain since they are outside the five senses and logic, and traditionally have been relegated to the category of mental illness. Without knowledge and support for these experiences, the person in the experience can feel disoriented and "crazy." However, if these phenomena are allowed to emerge for purposes of understanding and healing, these experiences have positive potential. Types of spiritual emergencies may include such experiences as the awakening of the kundalini (energy centered in the base of the spine), psychic opening, past-life memories, communications with spirit guides and "channeling," near-death experiences, and possession states.

Assagioli (1989) and Kornfield (1989) discussed expectations for those who practice meditation and other "self-realization" practices. It is not unusual for there to be events and experiences that are psychologically disorienting. These experiences are related to evolution of the soul consciousness. Some of the direct experiences may need guidance and psychological integration. According to Llewellyn Vaughn-Lee,

> when it comes to the esoteric aspect [of spirituality]—the inner teachings of a spiritual tradition such as breathing techniques, mantras, and visualizations that can awaken powerful inner forces, and that used to be kept secret except to initiates—these must be done in accordance with the spiritual tradition to which they belong, under the guidance of a teacher. Otherwise, they can be harmful. For example, kundalini energy or other psychic forces can be activated before the student is ready, causing imbalance or psychological damage. (Matousek, 1998, pp. 44-45)

Can therapists be trained to be present with persons who are undergoing psychological distress related to spiritual deepening, or should a spiritual guide, meditation teacher, or a spiritual director be present?

Table 5.1. Comparison of Depression and Dark Night of the Soul

Depression	*Dark Night of the Soul*
little spiritual connection	outgrowth of spiritual journey
sense of worthlessness	sense of unworthiness in presence of the divine
few spiritual insights	spiritual insights may be overwhelming
sense of inappropriate guilt	sense of appropriate guilt
little sense of blessings	can cultivate sense of blessings and grace
response to emptiness, hopelessness	response to spiritual fullness and letdown

NOTE: From Bullis, 1996, p. 120.

Minimally, counselors need to be able to distinguish between true psychosis and spiritual emergency, so as not to treat the latter with psychiatric interventions (drugs, hospitalization). Ultimately, the question is whether or not these spiritual experiences are being integrated into self or harming self. Support systems are important.

A Spiritual Emergence Network exists in California and operates as an information source for support and referral of persons going through spiritual emergencies (Waldman, 1992). Treatment includes experiential therapies, for example, Holotropic Breathwork, dream work, movement therapies, and spiritual practices, that facilitate a process toward a goal of healing and integration. Sometimes it is not appropriate to engage in transpersonal therapies, in which case clients are invited to do grounding activities to slow down the process so that they can "be in the world." Grounding activities include dietary changes and physical labor such as gardening.

Bullis (1996) distinguished between natural spiritual processes and psychological disorders, such as differentiating between depression and the "dark night of the soul," and between schizophrenia (psychosis) and spiritual awakening (see Table 5.1): "The dark night has but one cause—the spiritual cleansing of the self prior to a deeper, more direct experience with the divine" (p. 120). It may also involve a deep questioning of faith, which results in reaffirming it at a new level. He also compares the symptoms of schizophrenia with mysticism (see Table 5.2).

Bullis (1996) also offers some interesting insights on cults. The word *cult* means "a work of labor" and is derived from the same root as *cultivate* (p. 110). It refers to the process of cultivating a worship experi-

Table 5.2. Comparison of Schizophrenia and Mysticism

Schizophrenia	*Mysticism*
Disorienting or disconnecting	Meaningful inner and outer worlds
Isolation and alienation	Social relationships & boundaries
Escapism from social world	Social contact that is meaningful
Little involvement in social world	Training and guidance
	Goal of unity with divine, return to give back to social world

NOTE: From Bullis, 1996, pp. 118-119.

ence or altered state of consciousness. All religions have some "cultic activities" such as rituals (communion, calling the four directions), sacraments, beliefs, and creeds, and religious leaders with varying degrees of charisma. A feature distinguishing cults from religions is that a religion has a longer history and tradition in the world and has an open relationship with the world (its practices, beliefs). Cults, on the other hand, tend to gravitate around a charismatic leader and focus on a closed group membership through beliefs, group norms, group cohesiveness, and social isolation (Galanter, 1996). Early Christianity probably was considered a cult before it became politically recognized. Today, the word *cult* is used to describe any religious group that is nontraditional and threatening to the religious status quo. Bullis (1996) cautions readers about making judgments about cults. He suggests that the only way to make an accurate assessment of whether or not a cult is healthy for an individual is to examine the impact of participation on the individual through a process of spiritual discernment (examining the results or fruits of participation).

Cross-cultural examples of negative spirituality include spirit possession or soul loss. For example, in a medical case, a Hmong child was diagnosed with epilepsy by Western medicine. According to Hmong tradition, however, she had *qaug dab peg,* meaning "the spirit catches you and you fall down." Her illness was due to the wandering of her soul (Fadiman, 1997). Cases of spirit possession or loss may be found in other cultural frameworks and be included as part of a treatment plan, such as among Korean Americans (Yi, 1998) and Latin Americans (Centro San Bonifacio, 1997).

Rather than presume an either/or relationship, we propose that psychological health and spiritual health may be coexistent and collaborative rather than competing models. Frequently, counselors are in the business of supporting ego development. A healthily functioning ego can be used constructively for spiritual growth, and spiritual growth can enhance the ego (although in Eastern terms, it supersedes the ego: "the ego is a good servant, not a good master").

References

American Psychiatric Association. (1994). *Diagnostic and statistical manual of mental disorders* (4th ed.). Washington, DC: Author.

American Psychiatric Association. (1998, December). [Press release, Washington, DC.]

Assagioli, R. (1989). Self-realization and psychological disturbances. In S. Grof & C. Grof (Eds.), *Spiritual emergency: When personal transformation becomes a crisis* (pp. 27-48). New York: G. P. Putnam.

Ballentine, S. R. R., & Ajaya, S. (1981). *Yoga and psychotherapy: The evolution of consciousness.* Honesdale, PA: The Himalayan International Institute of Yoga Science and Philosophy.

Barret, R., & Barzan, R. (1996). Spiritual experiences of gay men and lesbians. *Counseling and Values, 41,* 4-15.

Battista, J. R. (1996). Offensive spirituality and spiritual defenses. In B. W. Scotton, A. B. Chinen, & J. R. Battista (Eds.), *Textbook of transpersonal psychiatry and psychology* (pp. 250-260). New York: Basic Books.

Bullis, R. K. (1996). *Spirituality in social work practice.* Washington, DC: Taylor & Francis.

Centro San Bonifacio, Erie Family Health Center. (1997). *Nuestra cultura, nuestra salud: A handbook on Latin American health beliefs and practices.* Chicago: University of Illinois at Chicago Press.

Chandler, C. K., Holden, J. M., & Kolander, C. A. (1992). Counseling for spiritual wellness: Theory and practice. *Journal of Counseling & Development, 71,* 168-175.

Clinebell, H. (1995). *Counseling for spiritually empowered wholeness: A hope-centered approach.* New York: Haworth Pastoral Press.

Cortright, B. (1997). *Psychotherapy and spirit: Theory and practice in transpersonal psychotherapy.* Albany: State University of New York Press.

Edwards, T. (1998). The heart of the matter. *Shalem News, 22*(2), 1-2. [Newsletter for Shalem Institute, Bethesda, MD]

Fadiman, A. (1997). *The spirit catches you and you fall down: A Hmong child, her American doctors, and the collision of two cultures.* New York: Farrar, Straus, & Giroux.

Fortunato, J. E. (1982). *Embracing the exile: Healing journeys of gay Christians.* New York: Harper & Row.

Frame, M. W. (1996). A social constructionist approach to counseling religious couples. *The Family Journal: Counseling and Therapy for Couples and Families, 4, 299-307.*

Galanter, M. (1996). Cults and charismatic group psychology. In E. P. Shafranske (Ed.), *Religion and the clinical practice of psychology* (pp. 269-296). Washington, DC: American Psychological Association.

Galland, C. (1990). *Longing for darkness: Tara and the Black madonna.* New York: Viking.

Gartner, J. (1996). Religious commitment, mental health, and prosocial behavior: A review of the empirical literature. In E. P. Shafranske (Ed.), *Religion and the clinical practice of psychology* (pp. 187-214). Washington, DC: American Psychological Association.

Grof, S., & Grof, C. (Eds.). (1989). *Spiritual emergency: When personal transformation becomes a crisis.* New York: G. P. Putnam.

Heise, R. G., & Steitz, J. A. (1991). Religious perfectionism versus spiritual growth. *Counseling and Values, 36,* 11-18.

Ingersoll, R. E. (1994). Spirituality, religion and counseling: Dimensions and relationships. *Counseling and Values, 38,* 98-112.

Ingersoll, R. E. (1998). Refining dimensions of spiritual wellness: A cross-traditional approach. *Counseling and Values, 42,* 156-165.

Judy, D. H. (1996). Transpersonal psychotherapy with religious persons. In B. W. Scotton, A. B. Chinen, & J. R. Battista (Eds.), *Textbook of transpersonal psychiatry and psychology* (pp. 293-301). New York: Basic Books.

Kelly, E. W. (1995). *Spirituality and religion in counseling and psychotherapy.* Alexandria, VA: American Counseling Association.

Kivel, P. (1991). Men, spirituality, and violence. *Creation Spirituality, 7*(4), 12-14, 50.

Koenig, H. G. (1997). *Is religion good for your health? The effects of religion on physical and mental health.* Binghamton, NY: Haworth Pastoral Press.

Kornfield, J. (1989). Obstacles and vicissitudes in spiritual practice. In S. Grof & C. Grof (Eds.), *Spiritual emergency: When personal transformation becomes a crisis* (pp. 137-169). New York: G. P. Putnam.

Matousek, M. (1998, July/August). Should you design your own religion? *Utne Reader,* p. 44.

May, G. G. (1982). *Care of mind, care of spirit.* New York: HarperCollins.

Morris, J. R., & Robinson, D. T. (1996). Community and Christianity in the Black church. *Counseling and Values, 41,* 59-69.

Myers, B. K. (1997). *Young children and spirituality.* New York: Routledge.

Pargament, K. I. (1996). Religious methods of coping: Resources for the conservation and transformation of significance. In E. P. Shafranske (Ed.), *Religion and the clinical practice of psychology* (pp. 215-239). Washington, DC: American Psychological Association.

Propst, L. R. (1996). Cognitive-behavioral therapy and the religious person. In E. P. Shafranske (Ed.), *Religion and the clinical practice of psychology* (pp. 391-407). Washington, DC: American Psychological Association.

Reilly, P. (1995). The religious wounding of women. *Creation Spirituality, 11*(1), 41-45.

Richards, P. S., & Bergin, A. E. (1997). *A spiritual strategy for counseling and psychotherapy.* Washington, DC: American Psychological Association.

Ritter, K. Y., & O'Neill, C. W. (1989). Moving through loss: The spiritual journey of gay men and lesbian women. *Journal of Counseling and Development, 68,* 9-15.

Ritter, K. Y., & O'Neill, C. W. (1996). *Righteous religion: Unmasking the illusions of fundamentalism and authoritarian Catholicism.* New York: Haworth Pastoral Press.

Waldman, M. (1992). The therapeutic alliance, kundalini, and spiritual/religious issues in counseling: The case of Julia. *The Journal of Transpersonal Psychology, 24,* 115-149.

Westgate, C. (1996). Spiritual wellness and depression. *Journal of Counseling & Development, 75,* 26-35.

Winell, M. (1993). *Leaving the fold: A guide for former fundamentalists and others leaving their religion.* Oakland, CA: New Harbinger.

Yi, K. (1998, October). Case report: Shin-byung (Divine disease) in a Korean woman. *Asian American Psychologist: Newsletter of the Asian American Psychology Association,* pp. 15-16.

6

Content Issues

EMPTYING AND RELEASING

> Grief has the potential to allow us to see how cramped we have always been. In acknowledging the pain, we can open past our long-held resistance to the unpleasant, to life itself.
>
> —Stephen Levine, in *Healing Into Life and Death* (1987, p. 111)

Matthew Fox (1983) has suggested that the spiritual journey may be experienced along four paths, "*via positiva, via negativa, via creativa, and via tranformativa.*" It is within this context that counseling concerns are explored as part of the spiritual journey. In the next two chapters, we will discuss four broadly defined counseling content areas that are frequently salient in people's spiritual journeys. In an attempt to retain balance, two content areas are associated more with pain and loss, and two are directed toward self-actualization.

The processes of releasing and replenishing balance each other, and both are pathways into deeper levels of self-understanding and spiritual awareness. This dance of destruction and creation emphasizes the concept that spirituality is not a unidirectional phenomenon. Therefore, this chapter focuses on the process of "emptying and releasing" and the next chapter focuses on the process of "filling and fulfilling." The process of emptying and releasing will reflect upon the themes of "making meaning of suffering, facing death, dying, and grief." Life's painful experiences create opportunities for in-depth exploration of spirituality in a search for strength and answers. In the next chapter, the process of filling and fulfilling will look at themes of "power, control, empowerment, creativity, and healing." Self-actualization requires similar soul-searching and accessing of energies that may otherwise be outside of one's awareness.

Although we make an arbitrary distinction between what seem like negative and positive processes, they are not necessarily that "pure." Both are equally important parts of the fabric of life. They are interconnected and may occur simultaneously or in what appears to be reverse order (e.g., one could contact creative energy and then grieve). Each theme area will conclude with personal reflection exercises for counselor personal awareness.

Making Meaning of Suffering

The story of the Buddha's life takes us back to India around the year 600 B.C. (Fields, 1992). As a son of a wealthy nobleman, Siddharta Guatama had not known suffering until as a young person he saw disease and the effects of aging for the first time. He vowed to seek the meaning of suffering and pursued a path that navigated the extremes of asceticism and diligent study, finally reaching enlightenment at age 35 and becoming known as the Buddha (the Enlightened One). He continued to teach for the next 45 years of his life. The Buddha's teachings have been translated into the Four Noble Truths, which provide an explanation for suffering, and the Noble Eightfold Path as a means of coping with and transcending suffering. Perhaps the most profound tenet of Buddhism is to recognize that life involves suffering (through attachments and desires) because the nature of existence is temporary and ever changing. See Chapter 2 for more discussion of Buddhism.

Cortright (1997) notes that the causes of human problems are ignorance, impurity, and unconsciousness due to conditioned identification with one's outer nature (a function of ego identification). From this perspective, it is one's lack of consciousness or awareness of one's spiritual nature that is a source of human suffering and pain. "Entranced by the outward looking mind and senses, our identification with the contents of

Box 6.1

Case Example

Shu-mei's younger brother died in a car accident when he was 17 years old. Shu-mei was close to him and had always watched out for her "baby brother." Shu-mei suffered intensely at his death and was not able to make meaning of his death until years later. Counselors frequently see clients only for a short period of time. It is not reasonable to expect resolution of the "why" question in a brief encounter, although the counselor can empathize with the pain and support the search for meaning. What sorts of meaning have you made of accidental deaths, and how are your beliefs shaped by your family's cultural background? How might you proceed with this client?

consciousness, our feelings, sensations, and thoughts, keeps us ignorant of our true nature, pure spirit" (p. 32).

Coping with pain and making meaning of suffering has been a central theme in counseling and psychotherapy. Finding meaning in suffering gives people purpose and is important for survival (Frankl, 1959). Sometimes there is a tension between belief in a loving, caring God and understanding why there is human suffering. Religious traditions often support the idea of a loving divine spirit that is capable of being present during times of suffering, such as invoking the Virgin Mary in the Catholic tradition. (See Box 6.1.)

Culture mediates pain and suffering. In the United States of America, which values freedom and the pursuit of happiness, people expect that life should be free of suffering. Due to their expectation of abundance in a middle-class lifestyle, suffering sometimes takes people by surprise. In contrast, suffering is acknowledged as a way of life in much of the nonindustrialized world, and pain is expected and "must be endured in silence" (Kleinman, 1988). For example, the Garifuna culture is an ethnic group on Guatemala's Caribbean coast and a culture of mixed influences (West African, Spanish, and Indigenous). According to one local source, when a baby is born the community mourns because they know what suffering lies ahead. When someone dies, however, they celebrate because the person is released from suffering (J. Davis, personal communication, July 24, 1998). The Shoshone Indians also have expressed a similar sentiment in their greetings upon the birth of a child, something like "my condolences," because they know how hard life will be.

Culture defines and gives meaning to symptoms and physical disorders. For example, various conditions may be called "complaints of 'soul loss' (susto) among working-class Mexican Americans in Los Angeles, spirit possession among Puerto Ricans in New York, voodoo among Haitian immigrants in Boston, 'airs' (aires) and hot/cold imbalance among working class Cubans in Miami, and evil eye among recent refugees from Latin America" (Kleinman, 1988, p. 25). Other cultural examples include conditions such as PMS or menopausal complaints, which are more characteristic of White, middle-class North American women. Kleinman (1988) suggests that illness as suffering raises two fundamental questions in Western culture: "Why me?" and "What can be done?" (p. 29). Unfortunately, the scientific approach to illness does not address the deeper existential layers of meaning of disease for both individuals and society.

From a Western perspective that values mastery and control over nature (Katz, 1985), the concept of accepting "what is" seems antithetical to a pressing need to dominate and control worldly experiences. The technological achievements of a postmodern world are truly impressive, such as extensive medical knowledge, engineering that extends from the bottom of the ocean to outer space, and computer technology that connects the globe. However, it is often difficult to know how to integrate human nature and spirit with technology (e.g., living wills, assisted death, cloning). This creates a spiritual vacuum, so to speak, that is now beginning to be addressed (Kung & Jens, 1997).

Cultures that are closely related to the Earth (e.g., agrarian societies) accept the forces of nature that are beyond human control, such as storms, earthquakes, fires, the weather, and seasonal changes. Whether these factors are attributed to the "gods" or have scientific explanations, the fact remains that there are some things in life that are outside of one's personal control. People may attribute different causality to these forces. For instance, "Is it something I personally did that is causing this suffering? Who or what is to blame? How is suffering explained, and what can I do about it? Is it karma, destiny, or God's will?" (See Box 6.2.)

What else causes suffering besides "acts of God" or natural causes? Unfortunately, people seem to have endless ways of causing suffering for each other through human greed, hate, fear, and aggressiveness. Physical trauma, rape, and other acts of violence occur on a daily basis, whether individually (e.g., in domestic violence situations) or collectively (in war). Sexual abuse of children may be conceptualized as a form of spiritual wounding, which also needs healing (Ganje-Fling & McCarthy, 1996; Parker, Horton, & Watson, 1997; Reinert & Smith, 1997).

Box 6.2

Case Example

Beatrice was a 26-year-old White graduate student who had multiple physical problems related to birth defects. She was confined to a wheelchair and had to go through various medical treatments, including surgery, to maintain her health. She was a devout Catholic and felt that God helped her and her family to cope. However, it distressed her to hear from her religious peers a belief that God had caused her disability. Discuss the implications of these differing religious interpretations of disability.

One of the qualities of human nature seems to be that of "remembrance and revenge." Many reasons are used to promulgate acts of aggression and violence (ethnic genocide, pogroms, and political conflicts). Mental health workers can play key roles in recovery and healing from physical and psychic wounds inflicted within and between nations (Comas-Diaz, Lykes, & Alarcon, 1998)

In the United States, where individualism is a central organizing construct, people are quick to "blame the victim" in personal acts of violence. While sympathy may be generated for victims of floods, hurricanes, earthquakes, and other natural disasters, what kinds of reactions are generated when there is rioting in Los Angeles, rape in the military, or crime based in poverty? Indeed, even in the health care system, what are the attributions to such diseases as cancer, alcoholism, or other forms of disability?

If one subscribes to a rational worldview, one seeks reasonable explanations and feels distressed by the unfairness or senselessness of tragedy (Kushner, 1981). The "why" question may not be answerable, but the "how to respond" question opens a door to healing. Sometimes invoking a rational God does more harm than good. An example of a well-intentioned but unhelpful intervention was noted by Elliott (1995), who was told when he was a 12-year-old child that his parents' deaths were the result of "God's will." This early childhood loss contributed to unresolved angst that led him to search out answers to life's existential questions by seeking out "wise and spiritual people." His compilation of interviews provides a window through which to view life's most difficult questions. It is reasonable to facilitate people's questioning of, or anger at God as part of the search for new understandings following traumatic events.

Finally, it is important for counselors to remember that they "can't speak for God" (National Organization for Victim Assistance, 1997; Shelby & Tredinnick, 1995).

The AIDS epidemic, although a worldwide phenomenon of devastating proportions, was initially treated in the United States as a "gay man's disease," and some viewed it as "punishment from God." It continues to be a stigmatized disease to this day due to associations with sexuality and drug use. Virtually all countries are affected, and the World Health Organization estimates that nearly 30.6 million people are HIV positive or living with AIDS (World Health Organization, 1998). Populations that are increasingly affected by AIDS are: in the United States generally, women and persons of color; in Florida, heterosexuals and persons over the age of 50 (Broward County Health Department, 1998); and in the world, people in developing countries. Working with persons living with AIDS requires that counselors have compassion and sensitivity to the spiritual dimension.

Implications for Counselors

Wherever there are suffering, death, loss, and pain, counselors not only must deal with the intense emotional processes, but also attend to the "making meaning" of the suffering. Although it may be tempting for counselors to disclose their own personal beliefs, this should be done judiciously. What is more important is that clients receive support to pursue their own answers to the difficult question, "Why?"

After people recover from the initial stages of suffering (shock, pain, despair), they are able to see (in hindsight) certain benefits that they have gained from the experience. For example, when the heart is opened to suffering, it is also able to be more compassionate, loving, and joyful. Suffering wakes people to being more alive and brings them to a more present-moment awareness. Such benefits are self-realized, however; they are not acquired through persuasion or testimonials.

Depression is a common response to life's difficulties, and may mask anger, despair, loss of meaning, and a "spiritual void" (Westgate, 1996). Westgate found that empirical studies of depression and spiritual wellness pointed toward four dimensions that were relevant to depression: finding meaning in life, intrinsic values, positive relationship to transcendence, and participating in a spiritual community. As mentioned in Chapter 3, sometimes depression is a part of the spiritual journey and a precursor to a spiritual breakthrough.

Box 6.3

Self-Reflection Questions

Think of a way you have personally experienced suffering (physical, emotional, spiritual).

1. To what do you attribute the causes of this suffering?
2. What has helped to relieve your pain?
3. How have spiritual or religious practices helped or hindered your healing?
4. What have others done that has helped or hindered your healing?
5. What are the implications of this process for your work as a counselor?

Kierkegaard wrote of the "paradoxical duality" of the human condition—the conflict between animal finiteness and infinite spirituality. Wetzel (1984) suggested that when this duality is denied, depression results from unrealized potentials, and the spiritual self tends to be sacrificed. Further, when one does not take risks to mediate this inherent conflict or to accept the conflict, depression and anxiety are the result. To address this, spiritual existentialists promote treatment that opens one's mind to the internal spirit within each person, paradoxically accepting the divine and human limitations. (See Box 6.3.)

Death and Dying

Facing mortality makes people ask the hard questions and therefore, for most, helps them in their own spiritual journey. Unfortunately, this topic is frequently approached with fear and denial in the dominant culture in the United States. Death stirs many emotions, whether it is the issue of the death sentence, abortion, assisted suicide, or death at old age. We live in a youth-oriented, death-denying culture.

Death brings us to the border between known and unknown realities. It is a time when one is on the boundary of "finitude and transcendence"

(Bertman, 1998). It is an opportune, if not compelling, time during which people frequently need to talk about religious or spiritual matters (Smith, 1993). Counselors are advised to be accepting and nonjudgmental of clients' theological beliefs around issues related to death. Counselors need to assist clients to identify and access their religious and spiritual resources, which can aid them in dealing with death (Smith, 1993). Although most people experience existential anxiety around issues of death and dying, it is a time that can lead them toward healing, wholeness, and transformation (Bertman, 1998). In some cultures the separation between the living and the dead is nonexistent, and ghosts or spirits may have a felt presence with the living. This raises such questions as, "Is there life after death?" and, "What is the source of life?"

Afterlife

It is hoped that spiritual beliefs about the afterlife help people to cope with their mortality. Life after death has been a theme of importance to world religions (Coward, 1997; Obayashi, 1992). Beliefs about the afterlife vary from culture to culture, and will be summarized briefly from three perspectives: ancestor worship, Eastern religions, and Western religions.

Ancestor worship is common in African and Asian cultures and is predicated on the belief that humans have souls that continue after the biological death of the body. Bond (1992) described the beliefs and practices of the Yombe tribe of northern Zambia, which will be summarized briefly. From the worldview of the Yombe, people have three identities: biological, social, and spiritual. Their social identity (place in the community) determines the appropriate burial rites. Ancestors are believed to have an abiding interest in the social life of the community after their death: "There is the notion of social persistence, and thus the social persona of the deceased remains part of the world of the living, concerned with human affairs" (p. 4.). Because ancestral spirits are believed to have power and moral authority, rituals are conducted through a ritual practitioner to communicate with ancestors and understand their wishes. In this case, the "social order" is preserved even after biological death.

Ancestors may be remembered and honored in other ways besides worship. People live on "symbolically," for example, through memories, through descendants' lives, through storytelling, and through their work or generativity. Relationships with loved ones often do not end at death, and grief is a way of expressing the love that one feels for the deceased (Bertman, 1998).

In the Eastern religions (e.g., Hinduism, Buddhism), a unique belief is reincarnation, that is, the cycle of birth-death-rebirth. The life cycle is viewed as without beginning or end, despite biological death. The "law of karma" provides a thread of continuity between lives. Both good and bad thoughts and actions are recorded in memory and influence the impulses that come up over one's lifetimes. The "karmic memory traces from one life to the next [are carried by] the subtle body, which separates from the physical body at death" (Coward, 1997, p. 7). The concept of "free choice" then determines good or bad actions and a gradual evolution spiritually (Coward, 1997). One has the potential of advancing toward god status or declining toward animal or plant status. One is released from the birth and rebirth cycle through god realization or enlightenment (nirvana). "What matters is how one uses the circumstances that each life provides to work toward the ultimate afterlife of one's choice" (Hopkins, 1992, p. 154).

A common theme in the Western religions of Judaism (Segal, 1997), Christianity (Penelhum, 1997), and Islam (Kassis, 1997) is that life after death involves resurrection, judgment day, and eternal existence based upon good or evil (heaven or hell). The details of how this happens vary slightly between these three religions, which share similar origins in the Middle East. The concept of monotheism (vs. polytheism), an afterlife, and struggles between good and bad (God and the Devil) can be traced to an ancient religion called Zoroastrianism, founded in Persia around the fifth century B.C. (Hicks, 1975). In all three of these major religions, there are varying emphases within and between traditions, ranging from viewing God as all powerful judge to God as all powerful source of love and compassion.

Symbols of the afterlife from Western perspectives emphasize a hierarchical relationship between heaven, earth, and hell. Symbolic representations from Eastern perspectives focus more on the circularity of life and how both darkness and light are contained within the whole. Whatever one's concept of the afterlife, it is important for counselors to honor clients' beliefs, and to assist clients and their family members to make meaning of death whenever possible. It is hoped that one's beliefs about the afterlife provide solace in the face of death.

It is difficult to maintain an awareness of death as an immanent reality. People who have had a near death experience have found it to have a profound effect on their lives. This is described in the next section.

Near Death Experiences

The investigation of near death experiences has provided some concrete descriptions of what the afterlife might entail (Moody, 1975; Ring, 1984; Sabom, 1982). Five stages have been identified as common to persons who have been revived from the threshold of death: (a) feelings of peacefulness, tranquility, and painlessness; (b) an out-of-body experience; (c) floating into a dark tunnel or void; (d) encountering a brilliant, warm, and loving light; and (e) entering another realm (Davidson, 1991). For some people there may be a life review. Not all stages are experienced equally nor necessarily in linear order. The fifth and last stage is the least reported, but has been described as a place of beauty where one might meet deceased relatives. Although the validity of this theory has been debated, reports of near death experiences seem to indicate that they are experienced as quite real and have had a deep impact on those individuals involved.

Responses to Death

People have different reactions to death depending upon various beliefs about the afterlife. For example, a client who thought she would eventually see her deceased mother in heaven felt reassured. One who thought her mother's energy was dissipated back into the natural world felt calm. Another, who did not know what happened to her father's spirit, was depressed.

Death by suicide presents unique issues for those left behind. When a suicide happens, family and friends are left with conflicted feelings, frequently guilt and anger. From a religious perspective, some religions have a strong taboo against suicide, while others may view it as a meaningful attempt to exercise control over one's life (Scott, Fukuyama, Dunkel, & Griffin, 1992). Questioning beliefs in God or God's purpose may occur following an unexpected death such as suicide, as well as wondering what the ultimate effect will be for the deceased's soul. (See Box 6.4.)

"Right to die" issues are beginning to be addressed in addition to physician-assisted suicide. The roles of the physician and other health care providers at death are also being reconsidered. Medical personnel are asked to humanize the experience with patients and family members through a supportive, witnessing role versus a pressured "life by any

Box 6.4

Case Example

Antonio, a 20-year-old Latino, comes to counseling distressed by his father's suicide. The young man believes that his father's soul is condemned forever in hell. Part of his grief is that he believes that he will never see his father again. How do you respond to this belief, and how can you be supportive of his grief?

means" mentality. What are the circumstances that would allow for a compassionate death, and what is the counselor's role in assisting families who may be considering refusal of medical treatment for a terminally ill patient? Counselors may play an important role in clarifying ethical considerations and involvement of the patient in making decisions regarding medical treatment for the terminally ill (Farrugia, 1993).

The issue of abortion is also controversial from legal, political, and religious points of view. Modern medical technology has enabled early in utero viewing of the fetus, which has reinforced the concept of granting personhood status prior to birth. When does life begin? When does the soul enter the body? Jewish tradition would place the beginning of life with the first breath. The Catholic position is that life begins with the fertilization of the egg.

Grief associated with an abortion is an area of yet unacknowledged spiritual significance. Because the decision is often rushed, the client may be left with processing the feelings much later and after the fact. At times, when the decision is made during adolescence, the capacity of young women to process the complexities of the decision are not yet beyond dualistic thinking styles, for example, good-bad, "I committed murder." Processing these feelings is complicated by the high-level publicity about abortion clinics (ranging from picketing to bombings) and continual coverage in the press on legislative and judicial rulings on the issue. The current debate between the "right to life" and the "pro-choice" movements has pitted absolutist positions of viewing the fetus as an individual human versus a woman's right to control her reproductive processes (Nelson, 1983). We suggest that in this kind of situation there is no easy or painless decision. Issues of loss and grief are present no

Box 6.5

Case Example

Doris, a 35-year-old woman, seeks spiritual guidance from her minister for healing around an abortion that happened when she was a teenager. Together they plan a personalized healing ritual. What are the benefits of rituals around highly emotional issues?

matter which direction a woman chooses. Nelson (1983) supports taking a religious approach that acknowledges that "each problem pregnancy has its own uniqueness, its own moral tragedy, and its possible alternatives" (pp. 162-163). (See Box 6.5.)

On the other hand, the Yombe tribe of northern Zambia does not consider a newborn infant to be a part of their social community, and if it dies, it is not treated with the same burial rites as one who is established in the community (Bond, 1992): "The act of being born does not establish humanity" (p. 7). Until the infant is recognized through appropriate ritual acts, it is not a member of the social order. Similarly, the Mayans do not name a newborn infant for 40 days. This illustrates that although birth and death are universal, cultural responses vary. Cultural variations in grief responses will be discussed in the next section.

Grief Work

Because counselors often intervene with clients who are mourning, the grieving process will be discussed, including consideration of multicultural variations. People often seek counseling for the first time in their lives when they "lose" someone close to them. While grief work is sometimes centered around coming to terms with the loss in a developmental sequence (e.g., Kübler-Ross's model), it can also stimulate questions "for the living," including, "Why did this happen?" "Why didn't this happen to me?" "What does this mean for me now?" and "What is the meaning/purpose of living?" These questions underscore the need to make meaning of dying.

These questions can be a catalyst for a person's progression on a spiritual journey, thereby becoming a healing for the person in the process. Death can be a catalyst for integrating unclaimed parts of self. In addition, bereavement work is spiritual work for the surviving people to understand, accept, and come to terms with some of life's ultimate questions (Dershimer, 1990).

It is helpful for people who are grieving to seek out multidisciplinary resources, such as contacting a religious professional in addition to receiving psychological counseling or group support. Hospice programs frequently offer group work for both bereaved adults and children, and are an excellent resource. Hospice programs philosophically believe in providing support for patients and their families so that they can do the closure work needed to say goodbye. Other activities, such as art therapy, massage therapy, and spending time in nature, can be soothing. People in the intense periods of grief often need to feel nurtured.

The death of a child is a crisis for families, and the way children react to the death of a sibling is affected by how the parents deal with their feelings of grief (Schwab, 1997). In addition, children need specific guidance in dealing with death (Monahon, 1997; O'Halloran & Altmaier, 1996; Wolfelt, 1983).

Cultural expressions of grief vary within North American cultures (Irish, Lundquist, & Nelsen, 1993). Emotional expressions and funeral customs vary by class, religion, ethnicity, and family traditions. The following comments are not intended to be stereotypes, but reflect cultural group generalizations. Within each cultural group there are within-group variations. Anglo-American traditions are represented by stoicism, and emotional reserve is perceived as a sign of strength. The expression of grief may be considered a private matter. African American traditions are influenced by Western African heritage, with beliefs in the afterlife as "going home" to the spirit world, a place of rest and happiness. Funerals may be characterized by spontaneous spiritual expressions, music, and emotional eulogies (Barrett, 1995). Dixieland music has its origin in New Orleans as an accompaniment for wakes. Mexican tradition celebrates the Day of the Dead on November 1, All Souls' Day, and families commune with their dead relatives through visits to the graveyard and cooking their favorite foods (Greenleigh & Beimler, 1991).

Grief work is highly effective in groups. The following comments were shared in a group of college students, each of whom had lost a parent. The question of "afterlife" was discussed: "Were their parents in heaven, disbursed as energy back into the universe, reincarnated, or in limbo?" Beliefs about the afterlife ranged from "mother is near, even in death" to "I'll see her in heaven when I die." One group member saw her father in her dreams, and wondered if he was visiting her because "he came back to

Box 6.6

Self-Reflection Questions

1. What was your first encounter with death (loss of a pet, loved one)?
2. What messages did you receive about how to deal with that loss?
3. What is your concept of the afterlife?
4. How has your concept of the afterlife changed over time and what has influenced your thinking about this?
5. How do you process your feelings of grief?
6. What are your fears about death, dying, and grief?
7. Describe a metaphor that captures your impressions of death (e.g., it's like a butterfly emerging from a cocoon).
8. What are the implications of your experiences in this area for your counseling?

apologize." One student expressed her angst about the premature death of her mother by saying, "Life is like a delete button on a computer, one minute you are here, the next you are not."

In group work, feelings of abandonment, fear, guilt, anger, and sadness were contained and yet triggered in the atmosphere of shared hurt. The group members spontaneously engaged in spiritual searching, ranging from formally enrolling in a religion class, to going on a "spiritual quest" to reading books like *Conversations With God* (Walsch, 1996). Such examples illustrate the active searching process that is stimulated by confronting death. However, group leaders need to be sensitive to differences in religious beliefs, as some people who have differing religious beliefs may feel left out or resentful.

Bertman (1998) suggested that the time of death is a time for hope, healing, making meaning, humor, transcendence, and transformation. Awareness of death paradoxically can bring one into a more intense awareness of life itself. Use of the arts, humanities, poetry, rituals, and music are other ways to enhance the death and dying experience and to make it a time for "healing into wholeness" (Bertman, 1998). (See Box 6.6.)

References

Barrett, R. K. (1995). Contemporary African-American funeral rites and traditions. In L. A. DeSpelder & A. L. Strickland (Eds.), *The path ahead: Readings in death and dying* (pp. 80-92). Mountain View, CA: Mayfield.

Bertman, S. (1998, December). *Last rights/last rites: Meaning-making and decision-making at the end of life.* Presentation at the University of Florida, Gainesville.

Bond, G. C. (1992). Living with spirits: Death and afterlife in African religions. In H. Obayashi (Ed.), *Death and afterlife. Perspectives of world religions* (pp. 3-18). New York: Praeger.

Broward County Health Department. (1998). *AIDS/HIV in seniors aged 50 and older* [Brochure]. Ft. Lauderdale, FL: Author.

Comas-Diaz, L., Lykes, M. B., & Alarcon, R. D. (1998). Ethnic conflict and the psychology of liberation in Guatemala, Peru, and Puerto Rico. *American Psychologist, 53,* 778-792.

Cortright, B. (1997). *Psychotherapy and spirit: Theory and practice in transpersonal psychotherapy.* Albany: State University of New York Press.

Coward, H. (Ed.). (1997). *Life after death in world religions.* Maryknoll, NY: Orbis Books.

Davidson, A. M. (1991). *A pilot study of the relationship between the near-death experience and personality type.* Unpublished manuscript, University of Florida, Gainesville.

Dershimer, R. A. (1990). *Counseling the bereaved.* Elmsford, NY: Pergamon.

Elliott, W. (1995). *Tying rocks to clouds: Meetings and conversations with wise and spiritual people.* New York: Image Books.

Farrugia, D. (1993). Exploring the counselor's role in "right to die" decisions. *Counseling and Values, 37,* 61-70.

Fields, R. (1992). *How the swans came to the lake: A narrative history of Buddhism in America.* Boston: Shambhala.

Frankl, V. (1959). *Man's search for meaning.* New York: Washington Square.

Fox, M. (1983). *Original blessing.* Santa Fe, NM: Bear & Company.

Ganje-Fling, M. A., & McCarthy, P. (1996). Impact of childhood sexual abuse on client spiritual development: Counseling implications. *Journal of Counseling and Development, 74,* 253-258.

Greenleigh, J., & Beimler, R. R. (1991). *The Days of the Dead: Mexico's festival of communion with the departed.* San Francisco: Collins.

Hicks, J. (Ed). (1975). *The Persians.* New York: Time-Life Books.

Hopkins, T. J. (1992). Hindu views of death and afterlife. In H. Obayashi (Ed.), *Death and afterlife. Perspectives of world religions* (pp. 144-155). New York: Praeger.

Irish, D. P., Lundquist, K. F., & Nelsen, V. J. (Eds.). (1993). *Ethnic variations in dying, death, and grief: Diversity in universality.* Washington, DC: Taylor & Francis.

Kassis, H. (1997). Islam. In H. Coward (Ed.), *Life after death in world religions* (pp. 48-65). Maryknoll, NY: Orbis Books.

Katz, J. H. (1985). The sociopolitical nature of counseling. *The Counseling Psychologist, 13,* 615-638.

Kleinman, A. (1988). *The illness narratives: Suffering, healing, and the human condition.* New York: Basic Books.

Kung, H., & Jens, W. (1997). *Dying with dignity: A plea for personal responsibility.* New York: Continuum Publishing.

Kushner, H. (1981). *When bad things happen to good people.* New York: Schocken Books.

Levine, S. (1987). *Healing into life and death.* Garden City, NY: Anchor/Doubleday.

Monahon, C. (1997). *Children and trauma: A guide for parents and professionals.* San Francisco: Jossey-Bass.

Moody, R. A., Jr. (1975). *Life after life.* Covington, GA: Mockingbird.

National Organization for Victim Assistance. (1997). The spiritual dimension of trauma. In *Community crisis response team training manual* (2nd ed., pp. 9.1-9.31). Washington, DC: Author.

Nelson, J. B. (1983). *Between two gardens: Reflections on sexuality and religious experience.* New York: Pilgrim Press.

Obayashi, H. (Ed.). (1992). *Death and afterlife. Perspectives of world religions.* New York: Praeger.

O'Halloran, C. M., & Altmaier, E. M. (1996). Awareness of death among children: Does a life-threatening illness alter the process of discovery? *Journal of Counseling and Development, 74,* 259-262.

Parker, R. J., Horton, H. S., & Watson, T. (1997). Sarah's story: Using ritual therapy to address psychospiritual issues in treating survivors of childhood sexual abuse. *Counseling and Values, 42,* 41-54.

Penelhum, T. (1997). Christianity. In H. Coward (Ed.), *Life after death in world religions* (pp. 31-47). Maryknoll, NY: Orbis Books.

Reinert, D. F., & Smith, C. E. (1997). Childhood sexual abuse and female spiritual development. *Counseling and Values, 41,* 235-245.

Ring, K. (1984). *Heading toward omega.* New York: William Morrow.

Sabom, M. (1982). *Recollections of death.* New York: Simon & Schuster.

Schwab, R. (1997). Parental mourning and children's behavior. *Journal of Counseling & Development, 75,* 258-265.

Scott, J. E., Fukuyama, M. A., Dunkel, N. W., & Griffin, W. D. (1992). The trauma response team: Preparing staff to respond to student death. *NASPA Journal, 29,* 230-237.

Segal, E. (1997). Judaism. In H. Coward (Ed.), *Life after death in world religions* (pp. 11-30). Maryknoll, NY: Orbis Books.

Shelby, J. S., & Tredinnick, M. G. (1995). Crisis intervention with survivors of natural disaster: Lessons from Hurricane Andrew. *Journal of Counseling & Development, 73,* 491-497.

Smith, D. C. (1993). Exploring the religious-spiritual needs of the dying. *Counseling and Values, 37,* 71-77.

Walsch, N. D. (1996). *Conversations with God: An uncommon dialogue, Vol. 1.* New York: G. P. Putnam.

Westgate, C. (1996). Spiritual wellness and depression. *Journal of Counseling & Development, 75,* 26-35.

Wetzel, J. W. (1984). *Clinical handbook of depression.* New York: Gardner.

World Health Organization. (1998, June). *The report on the global HIV/AIDS epidemic.* New York: The Joint United Nations Programme on HIV/AIDs and the World Health Organization [On-line]. Available Internet: www.who.int/emc-hiv/global_report/data/globrep_e.pdf

Wolfelt, A. (1983). *Helping children cope with grief.* Muncie, IN: Accelerated Development.

7

Content Issues

FILLING AND FULFILLING

> You must have a room, or a certain hour or so a day, where you don't know what was in the newspapers that morning, you don't know who your friends are, you don't know what you owe anybody, you don't know what anybody owes to you. This is a place where you can simply experience and bring forth what you are and what you might be. This is the place of creative incubation. At first you may find that nothing happens there. But if you have a sacred place and use it, something eventually will happen.
>
> —Joseph Campbell, in *The Power of Myth*
> (Campbell & Moyers, 1988)

As a counterpoint to the themes of emptying and releasing that were discussed in the last chapter, we now explore the processes of filling and fulfilling as expressed through themes of power, control, empowerment, creativity, and healing. Recall that these are not discrete or separate processes. For example, when a person engages in a transformational process (e.g., becoming more empowered or tapping into dormant talents), feelings of grief or the releasing of fears may be triggered.

Power, Control, and Empowerment

In this section, we will define power, discuss the concept of privilege, and demonstrate how these issues are played out in relationships and in society (Fukuyama & Franklin, 1996). We will discuss the role of a "higher power" and spirituality in relation to empowerment.

Webster's dictionary defines *power* with such terms as "[the] ability to do or act; force, strength, authority, and influence." Power can be attained by job position (e.g., dean or director); social role, often determined by gender, race, sexual orientation, educational status (degrees), economic status (wealth), seniority; and systemic factors (e.g., hierarchy, history, tradition). Counselors and helpers have power ascribed to them through their professional roles (Guggenbuhl-Craig, 1998). Personal power taps into such things as charisma, personality, energy level, moral code, and self-esteem.

People often are not aware of themselves as powerful beings. People may be less aware of their impact when they don't feel personally powerful, even though they are in powerful social roles. For example, a supervisor has power (authority and evaluation) over a supervisee. Faculty have power (evaluation and grades) over students.

What happens when a supervisor or person in authority oversteps his or her role, such as asking a supervisee to do favors that are outside of the usual job or role description? Such situations are problematic when persons with less power do not feel that they can challenge their "superiors," even when such requests may be inappropriate or unethical. Unfortunately, there are instances of sexual abuse of power in interpersonal relationships that occur both in the workplace and in churches.

Power issues can also be expressed in systemic ways. For example, what happens when a CEO expresses a strong opinion about some issue, and then it becomes company policy? This may bypass the usual group decision-making mechanisms, which can lead to morale problems in the work group. It also has a negative impact on the workers' trust of their leaders.

Privilege is associated with power and race in society (McIntosh, 1992). It has both historic precedents and contemporary repercussions. A recent wire story on a report to President Clinton by a federally appointed Commission on Race stated that,

> We as a nation need to understand that whites tend to benefit, either unknowingly or consciously, from this country's history of white privilege. . . . Specifically, the board noted an "inferior and uncivilized" status given

> indigenous Indians, who were then rounded up and isolated; "constitutionally sanctioned" discrimination against black slaves and their descendants for hundreds of years; "marginalization" of Latinos through military conquest; a belief from the early 1900s that Asians were "a source of cheap labor," undeserving of owning land or having full citizenship rights; and "social exclusion, discrimination and disenfranchisement" that confronted immigrants from Ireland and Poland or those of Jewish, Catholic and Muslim religious faiths. (Ross, 1998)

Privileges are the concrete ways in which power is expressed, often unconsciously. A person from a nonprivileged group will be better able to comment on the privileges of the powerful group. Here are some examples:

- heterosexual privilege: walking hand in hand with your lover or partner in public
- White privilege: seeing positive role models in media and in contemporary (or historical) society
- women's privilege: taking maternity leave to stay at home with a newborn child
- men's privilege: walking on the street at night without fear of rape
- economic privilege: basic necessities like housing, food, and employment are taken for granted
- student privilege: using student-only recreation facilities or receiving student discounts

People sometimes feel guilty about having privileges. Sometimes people feel "entitled" to these privileges, and feel threatened if other groups desire them. Strong reactions occur when issues of justice and access to resources are challenged. People who feel oppressed are concerned with such issues as equal rights, access to resources, and dealing with prejudice and discrimination. However, when people perceive that they have to give up power or privilege for another person or group to gain it, there will be resistance. Systemically, this is known as "backlash."

Many people have power and privilege in some areas of life and not in others. The process of power and privilege is dynamic and multileveled, not dichotomous (Early, Nazario, & Steier, 1994). For example, some individuals may experience privilege through class membership, race, and education, but not through other factors, such as religious status, gender, or sexual orientation. However, many groups have significantly less power systemically, such as the status of African Americans in the United States.

What are the spiritual implications of power relationships? One way to respond to social inequities is to ask, "How can I use my power and privilege to better the situation for someone who does not have them?" People with power and privilege can be "allies" of persons with less power. For example, heterosexual allies are needed to counteract homophobia and heterosexism (Dalpes, Obear, & Scott, 1990). Whites need to understand both the benefits and costs of racism, and need to develop a positive White racial identity (Corbett & Woods, 1998). There are intrinsic rewards for persons with power who work on reducing oppression and equalizing privileges. Such benefits include letting go of the need to "be on top," decreased fear, improved human relations in community, increased compassion, and resolution of power conflicts between groups. These principles have been integrated into an "oppression sensitive therapy model" for work with individuals, families, and systems (Early, Nazario, & Steier, 1994). Further, as discussed in Chapter 4, one's commitment to social justice is a natural extension of spiritual consciousness.

What role does a transcendent power or spirituality have in relation to the human issues of power and control? Is it possible to be powerful and retain the values of humility, service, and surrendering to a higher good? God-energy by definition is powerful. When one's work is directly related to "God's work," there is a danger of an overinflated ego or of moral righteousness. Sometimes it seems that to engage in spiritual powers requires a counterbalance of letting go, so that spiritual energies are not corrupted by the ego. Invoking God's name for various intentions or goals lends power to the intention. For example, fasting for spiritual discipline can be empowering for discipline, but starving oneself for ego gratification is damaging to the body and psyche.

The experience of acknowledging one's powerlessness or lack of control over a situation is an important stage in recovery for substance abuse addictions in 12-step recovery programs (Hopson, 1996). It is through powerlessness that one reaches out for help from a transcendent power. Acknowledging one's limitations and turning trust over to a "higher power" or "inner source" is an essential part of the change process. It is, however, sometimes difficult for counselors to understand when clients appear to be overly dependent upon an external higher power. (See Box 7.1.)

Box 7.1

Case Example

Fred is a 59-year-old White male who comes from a rural, poor background. He is under doctor's care for high blood pressure and other complications due to poor diet, smoking, and physical injury. He is "non-compliant" with medical advice, and the medical social worker tries to get him to take more self-responsibility. However, his response is, "The Lord will take care of me." How might a counselor discuss the issue of "spiritual surrender" and "self-responsibility?"

Gerald May (1982) talks about willingness versus willfulness as part of spiritual unfoldment:

> But we can begin by saying that willingness implies a surrendering of one's self-separateness, an entering-into, an immersion in the deepest processes of life itself. It is a realization that one already is a part of some ultimate cosmic process and it is a commitment to participation in that process. In contrast, willfulness is the setting of oneself apart from the fundamental essence of life in an attempt to master, direct, control, or otherwise manipulate existence. More simply, willingness is saying yes to the mystery of being alive in each moment. Willfulness is saying no, or perhaps more commonly, "Yes, but . . ." (p. 6)

The process of empowerment is commonly discussed in work with disenfranchised groups, such as women's liberation, Black power, gay rights, and others. Power struggles on socioeconomic and political levels mirror individual empowerment issues. When one feels personally empowered, there is less need to feel in control (H. Steier, personal communication, March 4, 1998). Power "over" self and others is qualitatively different from power "through" self, such as being a vessel or instrument for higher good. In other words, spiritual empowerment may be an anti-

Box 7.2

Exercises/Questions for Personal Awareness

1. Think of some different ways you have experienced power, both internally and externally. Describe some of the qualities of felt power (physical, mental, and spiritual).
2. How is "control" different from power? How are these two phenomena related to each other?
3. How do you negotiate the territory between your sense of "ego" and "beyond ego" (transcendence)?
4. What are some implications of these issues for how you do counseling?

dote for powerlessness as measured by customary cultural standards (e.g., economic power, physical power, skin color). For example, Cuban American women healers have been ascribed spiritual power through their roles as *santeras* (Espin, 1997). However, we do not suggest that issues of social justice be ignored in lieu of spiritual empowerment, as in the case with some evangelical movements in Latin America. As discussed in Chapter 4, multicultural work, which is socially empowering, is also spiritually empowering and vice versa. (See Box 7.2.)

Sexual Power

Religion has a significant impact on sexuality. In the Judeo-Christian heritage, women's bodies were seen as unclean, the sexes were separated in worship (e.g., Jewish and Islamic traditions), and physical desires were regarded as impure by Western religious standards (Payer, 1993). Earlier matriarchal, Earth-based religions honored the female body and the Earth as a source of life, and fertility was worshipped (Stone, 1976).

The history of Western civilization has included themes of domination and control of women's bodies. An antimaterial world replaced the Earth-centered religions, and spirit and body were split from each other. The afterlife, with its focus on heaven and salvation, became more important than Earthly life. Salvation was mediated by a priest through the church, and organized religion played key roles in national politics. In addition, marriage was determined to be the only means of sanctifying sexuality, and marriage was modeled after a spiritual model of submission (woman to man, man to God). Celibacy was seen as the only moral alternative to marriage.

Although many religions dictated sexual morality and provided many rules and prohibitions, there were some religions that deified the body and viewed sexuality as an expression of spirituality; for example, kundalini and tantric forms of spirituality (Bullis, 1996). In Hinduism, one of the symbols of the union with God was the lingua, depicting the joining of masculine and feminine energies through sexual union. Ancient erotic art from India portrayed the gods and goddesses in human embrace (Lal, 1967). Early Middle Eastern mysticism described spirituality in terms of "ecstacy of union with god" (see Barks, 1995). In the Jewish faith, the Sabbath is a holy time to have sex with one's beloved. So, indeed, not all religions have desacralized sexuality in the name of God. Another contemporary view is that sexuality is closely tied to spirituality, and may be so expressed symbolically through dreams (Taylor, 1993).

In cultural contrast, Native American spirituality has been described as inclusive, in that all things are considered sacred (Tafoya, 1997). Sexuality and gender roles were seen on a continuum represented by a circle rather than limited by linear stages or rigid categories. Human growth and development were regarded as ever evolving in contrast to being labeled in reductionistic categories. In some Native American traditions, cross-gender roles and bisexuality were regarded positively (Brown, 1997).

Reimer (1991) described sex as a high order value in that it enhances other values, such as love or aggression. By itself, sex is neither good nor bad, but rather it is instrumental, capable of good (e.g., relational bonding) or evil (e.g., rape). As such, sex can be given both sacred and profane meanings.

Homosexuality has been regarded as a deviation and an "abomination" by literal religious Biblical interpretations. However, other interpretations have suggested that sexuality (including sexual orientation) is a gift from God to be embraced as part of the spiritual journey (Ayo & Craighead, 1997; Griffin, 1998; Nelson, 1983). For the counselor, it is important to assist clients to develop a positive sense of self and sexuality. (See Box 7.3.)

Box 7.3

Case Example

Aaron is a 23-year-old Black male of Jamaican parents; he grew up in the United States. He is religious and worships in a Southern Baptist church. He feels conflicted over his sexuality, with feelings of attraction toward men while he maintains serial relationships with women. He feels more shame about his homosexual urges than his heterosexual activities, although both are condemned by his church. He believes that God judges him and that he is bad. When this is explored further, however, he hears his father's voice judging him. How can the counselor help the client "to discern" what is "right" spiritually, even though that might differ from conventional social mores?

A discussion of sexuality leads quite naturally into exploring relationships, couples, and family dynamics. An in-depth review is not possible in this chapter. However, the marriage and family literature is also examining the role of spirituality in relationships and its connection to therapy (see Brothers, 1992; Frame, 1996; Prest & Keller, 1993; Stander, Piercy, MacKinnon, & Helmeke, 1994). (See Box 7.4.)

Work Power

Expectations around work and career vary by class, educational level, and cultural background. Economic power contributes toward feelings of personal power and effectiveness in the United States. The Protestant work ethic affects self-esteem and social status in both employed and unemployed. The values of White-Anglo-Saxon-Protestant culture connect work and productivity with mental health and moral righteousness. Recent writers are exploring the relationship of spirituality and work (Bloch & Richmond, 1997; Hansen, 1997). Huntley (1997) suggested that work has four meanings from a theological perspective: "as a necessity, as good in itself, as vocation, and as co-creation" (p. 117). As the globe moves into the information era, however, rapid change challenges theological systems that were predicated on a hierarchical model. More peo-

Box 7.4

Exercises/Questions for Personal Awareness

1. How have spiritual and/or religious beliefs and practices influenced your attitudes toward sexuality?
2. How have your attitudes changed (or not) over time, and what has influenced these changes?
3. What are your current limitations in terms of counseling clients on issues related to sexuality and sexual orientation?
4. If God were a SHE, what would she be saying about sexuality?
5. What are the implications of the exploration of these issues on your counseling?

ple are faced with unemployment and increased leisure time, which may lead to a remaking of the meaning of work and leisure (Bloch & Richmond, 1998).

One way to join spirituality with work is to match one's deepest yearning with a deeply felt need in the world (Buechner, 1993). In this combination, individual talents and passions are joined to meet a greater need in the world. Matthew Fox, a Catholic theologian, suggests that life and livelihood should not be separated (Fox, 1994). Hansen (1997) emphasizes the need to look for "work that needs doing in changing global contexts" (p. 19). In this case, work may not necessarily appear as a traditional career track, but rather be a heartfelt part of one's spiritual journey. By the same token, a routine job may be approached with a heartfelt attitude or mindful concentration, which qualitatively changes the experience.

How is spirituality expressed in the workplace? How does the work world attend to such principles of social responsibility as human rights, social justice, and preserving the environment (DePree, 1997; Hansen, 1997)? Work values are not expressed just through individuals, but through organizations such as institutions and corporations (Briskin, 1996; Herman, 1994; Marcic, 1997; Natale & Neher, 1997). How the workplace values people and manages change is critical to the overall well-being of each organization. Current trends in the corporate world to downsize have major implications for the lives of thousands of employees. In many cases, unemployment creates a crisis for families and communities. It may open a door to spiritual seeking, as people are forced to adapt creatively. In some cases, a rethinking of values and reevaluating of materialistic needs leads families to change their priorities and their expectations of the workplace (Pulley, 1997). Such situations have spawned numerous career books with spiritual dimensions (Boldt, 1993; Sinetar, 1989).

The way people approach their leisure life may also have a direct link to their spirituality. Leisure, defined as open, relaxed, and creative time, nurtures one's soul (L. Thornton, personal communication, August 3, 1998). The opportunity to disengage from "doing" is an essential bridge to one's creativity, which will be discussed in this next section.

Creativity and Healing

The introduction of creative processes into counseling typically involves the traditional art forms, such as music, dance, and the visual arts (Gladding, 1998). Whereas these modalities have value and are credible approaches to healing, in this section we are interested in the creative process itself, more than the medium or the product. Art therapy is its own professional discipline, and we do not intend this discussion to represent or supplant it. In this section we will discuss the importance of creative processes for nurturing spirituality as well as for healing.

Remen (1993) suggested that creativity and healing are connected. She suggested that most people process and perceive the world through one of three primary modalities: visual, auditory, or kinesthetic. Depending upon an individual's primary mode, he or she is more easily able to access creative expressions, such as through dance, music, sound, visual arts, imagery, poetry, and body movement. It is through participating in the creative processes that people become healed and whole. In addition, talk therapy has its limitations. Sometimes engaging in creative processes is soothing and facilitates mental and emotional shifts in clients. (See Box 7.5.)

Music (singing hymns and/or gospels, chanting, toning, playing instruments) has been used historically to express spirituality in a variety of ways, and also to heal the sick. Goldman (1996) has written about the healing qualities of sound and the effects of harmonics on creating vibrational changes in the body and psyche. Esoteric practices from the world

Box 7.5

Case Example

Rebecca is a 42-year-old artist who doodles while talking to her counselor. She intentionally uses her nondominant hand, which helps her to tap into her intuitive side. Doing something with her hands also helps her to stay present.

religions have incorporated chanting vowel sounds that evoke qualities of the Divine; for example, *om,* the universal sound from Sanskrit. Sounds are essential to the practice of other spiritual traditions, such as the Kabbala, the inner teachings of Judaism, shamanic journeying, Sufism, and Tibetan Buddhism. In the Protestant tradition, singing hymns has spiritual power. "Music is, and has always been, an uncluttered path to my heart and soul. My religious heritage is Lutheran, and where those roots are very deep and very alive are in songs" (Reimer, 1998).

Remen (1993) has suggested that all healers are, in a sense, wounded healers, and it is through shared pain that we make each other whole: "every one of us is wounded, and every one of us has healing power" (p. 351). She continues to explain what she means by healing: "Healing may not be so much about getting better as about letting go of everything that isn't you—all of the expectations, all of the beliefs—and becoming who you are. Not a better you, but a realer you" (p. 354). In her work with cancer patients, Remen assisted them also to contact their inner truth and honest feelings. The process of sharing among persons who were suffering from this disease allowed more emotional honesty and vulnerability than is typically reached in socially polite company. This level of sharing contributed to wholeness that, in and of itself, was healing, regardless of the individual's physical health status.

Creative activities have been promoted in hospital settings to work with patients' healing processes, such as the Arts in Medicine Program (Samuels & Lane, 1998). The creative arts have a healing effect not only for patients, but also on improving the hospital environment and preventing staff burnout (Graham-Poole, 1993; Graham-Poole, Lane, Kitakis, & Stacpoole, 1994, 1995).

Artistic expression not only emanates from a spiritual place, but it can take on spiritual meaning. Ceramic artist Feral Willcox (personal communication, December 7, 1998) eloquently expressed this point in her artist statement:

> To me, all art is sacred in the most general sense because it sets aside a visual experience from the ordinary. A work of art serves as a mantra by saying, "Pay attention first to this . . . and then to this and this and this. . . ." Focus attention first on what is framed, what is chosen as subject, what is made special, what is, in a way an altar. The function of craft, then is to bring the sacred experience of art into the ordinary—to infuse the ordinary with spirit, to make sacred the wall, table, floor, cloth, or teapot. By extension, all things become sacred and all actions are meditations. So, to make one unusual teapot becomes an act of the soul; it brings temple into home or office or street, and my work as an artist becomes vital and central to the human experience.

The following thoughts on the topic of "creativity and healing" were shared in an interview by a professional gestalt therapist of a watercolor artist who conducts workshops (A. Pais, personal communication, July 25, 1998). Creativity is a process of being in touch with a natural part of self that is nonverbal, intuitive, and creative. This process engages the self in a spontaneous way. It is about "getting lost." Getting lost means "letting go" of time, left-brain rational thinking, critical thoughts, and turning off that voice that constantly judges and interprets life. Getting lost may be accomplished through such activities as rhythmic motions, sounds, actions, chanting, carving, drawing, painting, or writing. The activity itself puts one in touch with an open creative process. It is important to focus on process and not the end result.

Why is it difficult to engage in the creative process, and why is it necessary for healing? The process of moving from the linear, rational, analytical mind to a place of "nothingness" is scary for most people. It means giving up control of thoughts. It means going beyond known ego limitations. It means letting go of or surrendering, to some extent, one's normal defense systems, protections, and beliefs. For perfectionists, it means being open to the possibility of making mistakes or being wrong. It means letting go of results. It means lifting, if even for a moment, one's critical and judging mind.

How does this process aid healing? Two things can happen as a result of releasing into this place. One may contact early blocks or wounding, and, simultaneously, one may contact a spiritual source. It is like meditation. When one engages at this level with self, "psychological stuff" comes up. When people get into a creative process, they will eventually go to that place where their creative urges were originally hurt. For example, perhaps a teacher criticized a young boy's picture because he didn't "color inside the lines," thereby suggesting that he could not do art correctly. There may be tears, grief, sadness, and anger when releasing these blocks. And by doing so, healing can happen.

Second, people get into contact with an inner source that doesn't change and that does not lie. People do not have to be afraid of this space. It is holistic and connected to a universal good. As one develops trust and gets to know this part of self, it becomes not only a source for problem solving, but also a place from which to live and heal.

This creative process is based on the following assumptions: that people are inherently good, that there is a core self that is a "truth-teller," that there is natural strength that connects to universal consciousness, that this core self doesn't change even during times of transition or death, and that this is a "wellspring" of creativity and healing. Perhaps another word for *core self* is *soul.* The creative process by its very nature is holistic, balancing, and directly connected to spirituality.

People who have the hardest time experiencing their own creativity are those who cannot let go of the "end result." Ironically, the end result usually gets better when one lets go of it.

> Accessing the creative power within can be difficult sometimes because we are inclined to judge what we are doing and believe that we're supposed to produce something perfect or professional. Surrendering to the process of creating also can be difficult because the terrain may not look familiar and we feel uncertain about where we are going and where the story ends. Being in a supportive environment that nourishes our self-expression . . . is how we help each other reclaim this healing. (Hjerpe, 1998)

The resistance one feels to the creative process may be similar to the resistances one encounters doing therapy and on the spiritual journey. Thus, the creative arts are useful as a concrete expression for healing and spiritual growth.

Julia Cameron (1996) has proposed a method to access this intuitive side of self through writing "morning pages," a process of stream-of-consciousness writing on a daily basis. She has provided a structured activity to tap into creativity, which has at its core a spiritual base. After one gets over the awkwardness of writing, a process of problem solving and insight evolves. Stream-of-consciousness writing is similar to blind-contour drawing (i.e., drawing without looking at the paper). "It's like an estuary, a rich breeding ground" for insight (A. Pais, personal communication, July 25, 1998).

These creative processes are like a vehicle. For instance, "It's not the pot I make, it's myself" (Bender, 1996). The Japanese have refined art and the martial arts to be like a meditation, such as archery or the tea ceremony. All of the language of engaging in creativity in this way parallels spiritual language, such as to surrender, to accept oneself as good, and to experience the peace that comes with the process.

Creative processes may be used for healing specific types of issues (Cohn, 1997; Longman, 1994). For example, multimedia art was invited from women and men survivors of childhood sexual and physical abuse, rape, and domestic violence for a "survivor's art exhibit" (Funderburk, 1998). This project involved a community "witnessing" of these traumas, a step considered to be essential for moving through the three stages of healing: disconnection, remembering and mourning, and reconnection (Herman, 1992). This art exhibit included the visual arts, ceramics, sculpture, poetry, and performance art during the opening reception. Participation in this project was healing for survivors in that it provided a safe space for expression, validation of the traumas, an opportunity to mourn with others through the art medium, and a vehicle to reconnect with self and others in a supportive community. It also was empowering in that the traumas were depathologized and the survivors' voices were heard, an important intervention at the systemic level (Funderburk, 1998).

There are ethical considerations when using art processes in counseling. Hammond and Gantt (1998) identified six major ethical considerations when including art processes in the counseling relationship:

1. They first define artwork done in counseling as equivalent to verbal communication, which needs to be protected by confidentiality within the limits of the law. The counselor needs to be able to make decisions about what artwork should be retained in clinical records, with some cautions about work that might be easily misinterpreted.
2. They suggest that placing all of a client's artwork in a clinical record may violate that client's right to privacy.
3. The work setting may dictate expectations about record keeping and use of art (e.g., in a school setting working with children) and may also influence "ownership" of the artwork.
4. Photographing a client's artwork requires written permission. Keeping records of the artwork needs to balance with the client's right to privacy, professional accountability, and liability.

5. Using artwork in public displays or for research purposes raises the question of therapeutic or harmful effects upon the client.
6. Finally, there may be some circumstances in which a counselor would need to consult with a trained art therapist, and counselors need to know their limits in working with artwork in a therapy setting.

Creative writing is another outlet for spiritual renewal and connection with self at a deeper level. Natalie Goldberg (1990) advises writers to "go for the jugular," that is, to write about where the energy is. "Otherwise," she says, "you'll spend all your time writing around whatever makes you nervous. It will probably be abstract, bland writing because you're avoiding the truth" (p. 4). Writing exercises and writing support groups often "prime the pump" for creative expression (Goldberg, 1990; Newman, 1993). Journal writing specifically for spiritual growth was developed by Christina Baldwin (1991) and was a useful tool in a course for graduate counseling students on this topic.

Poetry is another medium for creative writing and can be utilized in counseling, educational, and hospital settings (Fukuyama & Reid, 1996; Graham-Poole, 1996). Poems speak from the heart and soul of people's real-life experiences. A poem "cuts to the quick" of human struggles for freedom, justice, recognition, oppression, and power. As Audre Lorde (1984) said in her essay, "Poetry Is Not a Luxury,"

> The white fathers told us: I think, therefore I am. The Black mother within each of us—the poet—whispers in our dreams: I feel, therefore I can be free. Poetry coins the language to express and charter this revolutionary demand, the implementation of that freedom. (p. 38)

Part of the power in poetry comes from the unusual or unexpected juxtaposition of words and from its brevity. Poetry is also a way to disrupt the dominant culture's language patterns, which often do not include the experiences of culturally diverse peoples.

Sample Writing Exercises

1. Suggestions for writing lines for a poem include the following: Write from your own personal life experiences; use specific, descriptive language; use your native tongue if that feels more natural; think in terms of your senses (taste, hear, smell, feel, see).
2. As a writer, you are communicating scenes that elicit emotions, memories with as specific details as possible, in order to capture human qualities to

Box 7.6

Exercises/Questions for Personal Awareness

1. Describe an experience when you felt creative; what factors contributed toward making this happen?
2. What are the blocks to getting your creative juices flowing?
3. How is creativity related to healing?
4. How is healing related to creativity?
5. In what ways does your cultural background encourage or discourage creativity?
6. How does spirituality or religion influence your creativity?
7. What are the implications of your experiences in this area for your counseling?

gain empathy from the reader. Commit to writing a set number of times during the week for a minimum of 30 minutes at a time. An example of a free association exercise: Write continuously about an object or from a starter word, like *ice cream* (Newman, 1993).

3. A nondominant-hand writing exercise: Ask a question by writing it with your dominant hand, answer with your nondominant hand. This allows your intuitive side to have a voice. (See Box 7.6.)

References

Ayo, N., & Craighead, M. (1997). *Sacred marriage: The wisdom of the Song of Songs.* New York: Continuum Publishing.

Baldwin, C. (1991). *Life's companion: Journal writing as a spiritual quest.* New York: Bantam Books.

Barks, C. (1995). *The essential Rumi.* New York: HarperCollins.

Bender, S. (1996). *Everyday sacred: A woman's journey home.* New York: HarperSanFrancisco.

Bloch, D. P., & Richmond, L. J. (Eds.). (1997). *Connections between spirit and work in career development: New approaches and practical perspectives.* Palo Alto, CA: Davies-Black.

Bloch, D. P., & Richmond, L. J. (1998). *Finding the work you love, loving the work you have.* Palo Alto, CA: Davies-Black.

Boldt, L. G. (1993). *Zen and the art of making a living: A practical guide to creative career design.* New York: Penguin.

Briskin, A. (1996). *The stirring of soul in the workplace.* San Francisco: Jossey-Bass.

Brothers, B. J. (1992). Spirituality and couples: Heart and soul in the therapy process [Special Issue]. *Journal of Couples Therapy, 3.*

Brown, L. B. (Ed.). (1997). *Two spirit people: American Indian lesbian women and gay men.* Binghamton, NY: Harrington Park.

Buechner, F. (1993). *Wishful thinking.* San Francisco: Harper.

Bullis, R. K. (1996). *Spirituality in social work practice.* Washington, DC: Taylor & Francis.

Cameron, J. (1996). *The vein of gold: A journey to your creative heart.* New York: G. P. Putnam.

Campbell, J., & Moyers, B. (1988). *The power of myth.* Garden City, NY: Doubleday.

Cohn, T. (1997). Art as a healing force: Creativity, healing and spirituality. *Artweek, 28,* 15-17.

Corbett, M. M., & Woods, K. (1998, June). *Talking across race.* Workshop presented for the Department of Student Affairs at the University of Florida, Gainesville.

Dalpes, P., Obear, K., & Scott, J. (1990). *Unlearning racism: Workshop on developing White allies.* Workshop presented at the Association of College and University Housing Officials, Athens, GA.

DePree, M. (1997). *Leading without power.* San Francisco: Jossey-Bass.

Early, G., Nazario, A., & Steier, H. (1994, April). *Oppression sensitive family therapy: A health affirmative model.* Workshop presented at the American Orthopsychiatry Conference, Washington, D.C.

Espin, O. M. (1997). *Latina realities: Essays on healing, migration, and sexuality.* Boulder, CO: Westview.

Fox, M. (1994). *The reinvention of work: A new vision of livelihood for our time.* San Francisco: HarperSanFrancisco.

Frame, M. W. (1996). A social constructionist approach to counseling religious couples. *The Family Journal: Counseling and Therapy for Couples and Families, 4,* 299-307.

Fukuyama, M., & Franklin, L. (1996). Power, privilege and predicaments. *Student Affairs Update, 21*(3), 7.

Fukuyama, M. A., & Reid, A. D. (1996). The politics and poetry of multiculturalism. *Journal of Multicultural Counseling and Development, 24,* 82-88.

Funderburk, J. R. (1998, March). *The survivor's art exhibit: A feminist approach to healing and recovery.* Presentation at the Association of Women in Psychology National Conference, Baltimore, MD.

Gladding, S. T. (1998). *Counseling as an art: The creative arts in counseling* (2nd ed.). Alexandria, VA: American Counseling Association.

Goldberg, N. (1990). *Wild mind: Living the writer's life.* New York: Bantam Books.

Goldman, J. (1996). *Healing sounds: The power of harmonics.* Rockport, MA: Element Books.

Graham-Poole, J. (1993). A healthy society. *The Journal of the Healing Health Care Project, 2*(3), 28-30.

Graham-Poole, J. (1996). Children, death, and poetry. *Journal of Poetry Therapy, 9*(3), 129-141.

Graham-Poole, J., Lane, M. R., Kitakis, M. L., & Stacpoole, L. (1994). Creating an arts program in an academic medical setting. *International Journal of Arts Medicine, 3*(2), 17-25.

Graham-Poole, J., Lane, M. R., Kitakis, M. L., & Stacpoole, L. (1995). Re-storying lives, restoring selves: The arts and healing. *International Journal of Arts Medicine, 4*(1), 20-23.

Griffin, J. L. (1998). Exiles' return. *Common Boundary, 16*(3), 28-34.

Guggenbuhl-Craig, A. (1998). *Power in the helping professions* (2nd ed.). New York: Continuum Publishing.

Hammond, L. C., & Gantt, L. (1998). Using art in counseling: Ethical considerations. *Journal of Counseling and Development, 76,* 271-276.

Hansen, L. S. (1997). *Integrative life planning: Critical tasks for career development and changing life patterns.* San Francisco: Jossey-Bass.

Herman, J. L. (1992). *Trauma and recovery.* New York: Basic Books.

Herman, S. M. (1994). *The Tao at work.* San Francisco: Jossey-Bass.

Hjerpe, K. (1998, August). *Creative healing in art* [Sermon]. Gainesville, FL: United Church of Gainesville.

Hopson, R. E. (1996). The 12-step program. In E. P. Shafranske (Ed.), *Religion and the clinical practice of psychology* (pp. 533-558). Washington, DC: American Psychological Association.

Huntley, H. L. (1997). How does "God-talk" speak to the workplace?: An essay on the theology of work. In D. P. Bloch & L. J. Richmond (Eds.), *Connections between spirit and work in career development: New approaches and practical perspectives* (pp. 115-136). Palo Alto, CA: Davies-Black.

Lal, K. (1967). *The cult of desire* (2nd ed.). New Hyde Park, NY: University Books.

Longman, R. (1994). Creating art: Your Rx for health, part I and II. *American Artist, 58,* 68-70.

Lorde, A. (1984). *Sister outsider: Essays and speeches.* Trumansburg, NY: Crossing Press.

Marcic, D. (1997). *Managing with the wisdom of love: Uncovering virtue in people and organizations.* San Francisco: Jossey-Bass.

May, G. G. (1982). *Will and spirit: A contemplative psychology.* New York: Harper & Row.

McIntosh, P. (1992). White privilege and male privilege: A personal account of coming to see correspondences through work in women's studies. In M. Andersen & P. Hill Collins (Eds.), *Race, class and gender* (pp. 70-81). Belmont, CA: Wadsworth.

Natale, S. M., & Neher, J. C. (1997). Inspiriting the workplace: Developing a values-based management system. In D. P. Bloch & L. J. Richmond (Eds.), *Connections between spirit and work in career development: New approaches and practical perspectives* (pp. 237-255). Palo Alto, CA: Davies-Black.

Nelson, J. B. (1983). *Between two gardens: Reflections on sexuality and religious experience.* New York: Pilgrim Press.

Newman, L. (1993). *Writing from the heart. Inspiration and exercises for women who want to write.* Freedom, CA: Crossing Press.

Payer, P. (1993). *The bridling of desire.* Toronto: University of Toronto Press.

Prest, L. A., & Keller, J. F. (1993). Spirituality and family therapy: Spiritual beliefs, myths, and metaphors. *Journal of Marital and Family Therapy, 19,* 137-148.

Pulley, M. L. (1997). *Losing your job, reclaiming your soul.* San Francisco: Jossey-Bass.

Reimer, L. (1991, January). *Between two gardens: Spirituality and sexuality* [Sermon]. Gainesville, FL: United Church of Gainesville.

Reimer, S. (1998, December). *My song in the night* [Sermon]. Gainesville, FL: United Church of Gainesville.

Remen, R. N. (1993). Wholeness. In B. Moyers, B. S. Flowers, & D. Grubin (Eds.), *Healing and the mind* (pp. 343-363). Garden City, NY: Doubleday.

Ross, S. (1998). *"White privilege" rules, says board. Report to president urges more American education on racial diversity.* Washington, DC: Associated Press. [Associated Press release, Internet]

Samuels, M., & Lane, M. R. (1998). *Creative healing: How to heal yourself by tapping your hidden creativity.* San Francisco: HarperSanFrancisco.

Sinetar, M. (1989). *Do what you love, the money will follow: Discovering your right livelihood.* New York: Dell.

Stander, V., Piercy, F. P., MacKinnon, D., & Helmeke, K. (1994). Spirituality, religion and family therapy: Competing or complementary worlds. *The American Journal of Family Therapy, 22,* 27-41.

Stone, M. (1976). *When god was a woman.* New York: Harcourt Brace Jovanovich.

Tafoya, T. (1997). Native gay and lesbian issues: The two-spirited. In B. Greene (Ed.), *Ethnic and cultural diversity among lesbians and gay men* (pp. 1-10). Thousand Oaks, CA: Sage.

Taylor, J. (1993). *Where people fly and water runs uphill: Using dreams to tap the wisdom of the unconscious.* New York: Warner Books.

8

Process Issues

> Here is the mystery: If the rhythm is right, if the translation between inner mood and drum membrane is perfect, then you know it instantly. . . . When the rhythm is right you feel it with all your senses; it's in your mind, your body, in both places. . . . A feeling not unlike trust settles over you as you give yourself to the rhythm. You don't fight it, but instead allow yourself to be propelled by this insistent but friendly feeling. All sense of the present moment disappears, the normal categories of time become meaningless. Your mind is turned off, your judgment wholly emotional; you feel light, gravityless, your arms feel like feathers. You fly like a bird. . . . Up on stage, it's almost totally intuitive. The unexpected is still courted; magic won't happen unless you set a place at the table for it.
>
> —Mickey Hart, in *Drumming at the Edge of Magic: A Journey Into the Spirit of Percussion*

Introductory Comments

Though spirituality has been excluded from many traditional therapy approaches, mental health professionals recently have advocated a focus on both religion and spirituality (Cornett, 1998; Richards & Bergin, 1997). Spiritual dimensions such as making meaning, values, mortality, organization of the universe (worldview), suffering, and transcendence have been described as directly relevant to the "soul of psychotherapy" (Cornett, 1998). Taking this view, spirituality becomes integral to the process of therapeutic change and human growth.

Therapy is a time for change and transformation to happen, that is, transformation of the self (self-awareness), coming in touch with something outside of one's self or a higher power (transcendence), and gaining meaning in one's life (meaning making). Part of the spiritual process in therapy involves removing blocks to awareness, gaining a sense of transcendence, and developing meaning making, thereby providing an environment in which transformations can naturally occur. In this sense, the chapter's opening quote captures the essence of what integrating spirituality into multicultural counseling can provide, a deep awareness and an intuitive sense of flow, harmony, and connecting.

This chapter will focus on salient process issues that can occur when integrating spirituality and multiculturalism in counseling and therapy. The chapter will be organized around the following themes: counselor process, client process, client and counselor interaction themes, ethical considerations, and contraindications.

Tan (1996) suggests that there are two models for spiritual interventions in counseling: implicit and explicit integration of religion in clinical practice. In this chapter, we will discuss primarily an implicit integration of spirituality into the counseling process, not integrating religion per se. Counseling "process" is defined as interactions between counselor and client that indicate how the relationship is proceeding (Strupp & Binder, 1984). Process variables are relational, are mostly nonverbal, and involve expectations. Basically, everything that is not "content" becomes "process."

Given the focus on counseling process, we encourage the reader to keep in mind that process themes occur in all forms of counseling, in all settings, and within the context of multiple theoretical approaches. So, while various approaches might on the surface seem more amenable to integrating spirituality in therapy (e.g., existential approaches), the issues presented in this chapter are applicable to all theoretical approaches to counseling.

Counselor Process

Spiritual writers and teachers have long promoted that, in working with people, the content (mind) is one vehicle for interpersonal impact, but the transcendent (spiritual) qualities of people are equally important. The goal of therapy becomes to be able to see behind the words, behind the mask that people project (the apparent personality), and to see the true person. A key concept is that people have the "true" self within them. The problem is that via unhealthy socialization, damaging experiences, unrealistic expectations, and other traumatic experiences, the "true" self gets buried and other ("false") selves come forward.

In order to do this type of counseling work, it is helpful for counselors to be able to work on several levels at the same time to gain a sense of harmony, a sense of flow, and to become free from the trappings of the mind and the fear of projections. In other words, it is helpful when counselors can reach into their own true being—the true self—and access a level of being that is comfortable with the true self and not comfortable just with the personality that is projected. It is helpful when counselors can free themselves "to be" and not fall back on the safer routes of "doing" and "saying."

There can be fear due to the tenuousness of this situation. However, there is as much power as there is fear. A powerful way to open these doors involves tapping into the spiritual dimension of life. One way this plays itself out is in the relationship between two people and developing a "presence" (Korb, 1988). The impact of one being on another is great and meaningful. The challenge becomes how to translate this process into the counseling session or, indeed, into life itself. The power can be used to unleash and free wonderful qualities and can be a catalyst for rebirth for the client. In a sense, a transformation happens when this level is accessed. The goal is a transformation into what and who the client really is, which, of course, is what and who the client wants to be (Cortright, 1997).

Kelly (1995) described four areas that aid counselors in this transformation process: awareness, benevolent connectedness, unconditional and hopeful openness, and transcendent meaningfulness. There are times when the above areas are difficult to accomplish because counselors can be "addicted" to the mind level (to thoughts, ideas, concepts, attitudes) for various reasons (May, 1988). One reason is that this is usually a safer route through which to conduct daily business. Second, mental health professionals have been reinforced at the mind level in traditional training and practice. It is difficult to let go of one's usual cognitive processes. Involved in this letting go is the concept of surrendering or releasing. In spiritual language, the ego needs to surrender to let a higher power of life take over. This is done, in part, through self-acceptance, which is a necessary step before one can keep going on a spiritual journey. As counselors learn to listen to themselves and to others more deeply, access to this level of "true self" becomes more fully realized.

Counseling that integrates the spiritual dimension involves removing blocks to this process. There are specific techniques that help access this source—various forms of meditation, breathing techniques, and exercises in grounding and centering. It is important to remember these techniques are an everyday way of life for people in many cultures of the world. In addition, when counselors "authentically" (Kelly, 1995) integrate spirituality into their lives, they feel less need to talk about it in abstract terms and no desire to "change" people's beliefs. In contrast, they feel a greater need to understand, listen, and connect fully with the client.

The possibility of transformation and rebirth is always present. If counselors can be open to a process of expansion and contraction in consciousness, and safer routes of existence do not block this process, then a trusting environment is created. Counselors need to be open to and accepting of what might happen before clients will be able to do this in therapy. As counselors accomplish this, they will access the true vitality of life and see the strength of human faith and of the human spirit in action. The concept of *being,* drawn from humanistic writers, is integral in this process. In other words, the helper has to be relatively secure in his or her own *being.*

For example, counseling involving bereavement brings forth spiritual dimensions for counselor and client alike. It is quite possible that clients come to counselors who have not thought through what death means to them, what life means to them, or what "happens" after death. However, if counselors can be relatively secure in what knowledge they do have, in what knowledge they do not, and if other relational variables are present (e.g,, emotional connectedness, empathy, compassion, mindfulness), this security will be translated to the client. The desired effect, for both counselor and client, is that one does not need to "know everything." What is needed is to be comfortable being at whatever point one is on the continuing journey.

A potentially useful indicator of this "comfortableness" is one's self-assessment of identity development. As mentioned in Chapter 3, a model of identity development that is helpful for looking at the integration of spiritually into psychological development and multicultural development is the OTAID model. Theoretically, the higher one's identity development, the more comfortable one becomes with one's self and with others. In the latter phases, an interconnection of all life is seen and valued, and a spiritual connection with all is felt. Inherent in this is self-valuing as well as self-knowledge. As mentioned previously, the SII can be used to assess a person's relative strength at each stage in the OTAID model.

The role of self-disclosure becomes important when integrating spirituality into multicultural counseling. Much research in the fields of psychotherapy and multicultural counseling has pointed to the therapeutic effects of self-disclosure. In addition, self-disclosure is seen as important in the practice of spiritual direction (Healey, 1990). Self-disclosure is also seen as an important variable in building and maintaining the therapeutic relationship, in developing trust between counselor and client, and for therapeutic change itself. It can also help manifest the connection and interconnection between counselor and client. It can also provide a client with a direction in which he or she has not gone, which may be helpful. When discussing spiritual issues with a client, it is obviously important for counselors to refrain from self-disclosing in a way that promotes their own views and beliefs, blatantly or in a more subtle fashion, at the expense of the client's.

Client Process

Oftentimes, before a change or transformation takes place, there is a good deal of accompanying anxiety, and a client may be resistant to the impending change. This can be a frightening and scary time, filled with unknowns. In short, this is usually a crisis time (to a lesser or greater degree) for most clients, a crisis time in the faith and meaning that they have constructed for themselves. The Chinese word for crisis is translated as "dangerous opportunity." The danger is present in the intense feelings that people have and the possible consequences of these feelings. The opportunity is that the time in one's life combined with the surrounding events can be a powerful impetus for change. As one client said, "Thanks for pointing me in the direction of the opportunity that was buried within my crisis."

People try so hard to hold on to the past, to the old way of doing things, that they feel drained because of all the energy this takes. At some point (and often due to an external pressure), there is a realization that a new system needs to be gained. So, it is time to say goodbye to "old friends," to let the old part die, to accept what it has given, and to move on. It is time for transformation, for a new season, for rebirth to a new level of consciousness and awareness. For some clients, this means becoming more authentic and increasing self-awareness and self-knowledge. Again, it is therapeutic when people are encouraged to express their authentic selves. People need to be comfortable with an evolving self, or, as one client put it, "I feel like a totally new person since last year and am making many changes."

For other clients, it means increasing awareness of certain cognitive patterns and styles that are no longer adaptive. In fact, cognitive therapy is a natural bridge for integrating spirituality into the counseling process. Many beliefs people have are rooted in how they make meaning of life, expectations they have of themselves and others, and their goals for the future. Encouraging clients to increase awareness of other ways to view these areas (i.e., cognitive restructuring) can help address their anxiety and depression.

As it is with counselor processes and issues, finding one's place on the identity development path using the OTAID model can be helpful for clients. Again, identity development models and theories offer a glimpse of where one might be on this path and where one might want to go in the future. In the OTAID model, self-knowledge and acceptance of one's true self are seen as one attainable goal of an intentional identity development process.

It is difficult to describe in words what a spiritual therapeutic process feels like, but Box 8.1 descriptively illustrates a particularly meaningful counseling session wherein some of these spiritual dimensions were tapped. The words come from a client who was dealing with bulimia and struggling with how to talk with her parents about her illness, as well as about family issues in general.

Client and Counselor Interaction

This section will briefly address themes and issues surrounding the counselor-client interactions that arise when working from a spiritual base. Basic spiritual values, such as connectedness of all beings, compassion, forgiveness, and respect, all help the counseling dyad toward the goal of affirming human dignity and diversity as a vital part of existence and a vital part of becoming "who one is." This general concept of "acceptance" fits with multicultural counseling concepts of trying to understand a person's frame of reference when it is not one's own, seeing multiple perspectives, and seeing the "other" in authentic, "nonstereotypical" ways.

Kelly (1995) describes counseling as having two main components: the relationship and the technical tools. Independent of theoretical orientation, the counseling relationship is important (Gelso & Carter, 1985).

Box 8.1

A Client's Thoughts

Client's thoughts following a spiritually meaningful counseling session:

- connection with counselor at deep level
- transformation into what she wanted
- scared, not sure, unknown territory
- freeing—bird out of a cage
- energy
- being who she really was
- wanted to share with others
- responsibility for self—not totally for others
- more flowing, spontaneous; not censoring
- self-confidence is a positive form of protection
- risk, tenuous
- very present
- risk and responsibility
- not knowing where it is going, some fear in this
- cannot go back to way she used to be

When one engages in the counseling relationship, issues such as power, authority, expectations, and control start to emerge. The central point we want to make here is that an implicit spiritual backdrop may help to navigate the "tricky" parts of the counseling relationship and help to bring forth the positive functions of this unique relationship.

In enacting this approach, boundary issues between counselor and client become important for the counselor. It is helpful to keep the roles of counselor and client steady while behaving in a way that is respectful and genuine.

Countertransference issues also become important for the counselor. At times, what the client presents will trigger feelings and thoughts in the counselor, often deep rooted and, at times, unexamined. What is important to remember when this happens is that there is no substitute for awareness and examination of the counselor's own beliefs and values surrounding spirituality and religion. As in all countertransference situations, guidelines for addressing these situations include:

What does the client say or do that triggers the counselor's reactions?

What are the counselor's personal beliefs that interfere with working with this client?

What current situations outside of therapy are affecting work with this client?

Ethical Considerations

There are several ethical issues to take into account when integrating spirituality in multicultural counseling. Ganje-Fling and McCarthy (1996) have identified five general areas for consideration:

Premature Spiritual Interventions

At times, the psychological aspects of presenting issues need to be dealt with before any exploration of the spiritual domain takes place. For example, issues surrounding recent sexual assault, becoming aware of childhood abuse, or crisis issues often need psychological intervention before the client is ready to discuss the deeper and contextual issues. In addition, it is helpful to discuss spiritual issues only after a trusting relationship has been established. Since society in general struggles over discussing spiritual issues openly, most clients struggle with this and need to feel safe before opening up.

Blurring of Boundaries

Should counselors be talking about religious or spiritual matters? Is this a role violation with ministers or priests or rabbis or spiritual directors? Before spiritual interventions are undertaken, it is recommended that a thorough assessment be conducted in which the nature of the presenting issues is made clear, knowledge is gained about the person's support system, and a counseling relationship begins to be established. A general question about spiritual or religious background could be included in the assessment and returned to later in therapy if pertinent.

Countertransference

As mentioned above, a main responsibility of the counselor is to make sure his or her personal needs are not being enacted. For example, counselors should not take this opportunity to proselytize personal spiritual views or conflicts. Caution is indicated about counselor self-disclosure, as mentioned above, because clients may view counselors as judgmental and not disclose their beliefs. In addition, counselors may become less effective if their views and clients' views are too similar or too dissimilar.

Referral to Religious Professionals

It is important and indeed ethical to be aware of one's limits when dealing with particular issues and to know when to refer a client for additional help, including "adjunct therapy." The same is true for spiritual issues. Oftentimes the counseling process is helped when a client can talk with someone from his or her own religious faith for guidance on a particular issue. The opposite also can be true: At times it would not be helpful, and in some cases damaging, to talk with religious leaders. Again, knowing the client and the presenting issue will guide this decision-making process.

Lack of Training

For most mental health professionals trained in traditional social work, counseling, or psychology programs, there is a lack of preparation and lack of supervision for spiritual issues. While personal journeying and development are important, it is also important to have received some training in working with spiritual issues in therapy before embarking on this with clients. Ongoing supervision in some fashion is just as important as with other therapeutic issues.

An area of continued dialogue and concern is the issue of separation of church and state. This is a particular concern in the public school systems, and federal guidelines have been delineated. These guidelines will be summarized here because they are an attempt to honor religious freedom without imposition of values, a difficult boundary for most people (and institutions) to negotiate.

Box 8.2

Case Example

Carol, a physician's assistant who worked in a public health clinic, would ask her patients if they wanted her to pray with them to help heal their illnesses. Frequently, the patients who were from poor rural backgrounds were grateful for this gesture of concern. However, her supervisor did not approve. What are the ethical considerations and boundary issues in this case?

Teachers, administrators, and other school officials are prohibited from organizing prayers or advocating either religious or antireligious views. They are advised to treat religious activities in the same way as other nonacademic activities are treated; for example, religious groups may be allowed to use school facilities according to the same guidelines as other groups. However, no religious activity is allowed that involves harassment or coercion of people to participate. The guidelines do allow for individual or group prayer if it is nondisruptive, and for student-initiated religious discussions. Religious activities may also be scheduled before or after school, such as reading religious scriptures. Wearing religious symbols is also allowed ("School Guidelines," 1995).

Consideration of work setting and context will likely influence the degree to which counselors may integrate spiritual and religious dimensions into their work. Obviously, counselors in private practice have different liberties in presenting their counseling orientation than do practitioners working in the public sector (e.g., in VA hospitals). (See Box 8.2.)

What is prayer and why is it such a sensitive issue; for example, the controversy over prayer in schools. Prayer is an activity directed toward the Ultimate and an invocation of transcendent power. At times, it may be considered communication with an inner self or listening for intuition. There are different types of prayers, including prayers of petition (asking), praise, confession, thanksgiving, intercession on behalf of others, and different types of meditation or contemplative practices, such as emptying, insight, centering, and focused attention (Simpkinson & Simpkinson, 1998). There is some evidence to show that intercessory prayer has positive effects on patients' recovery from illness (Sicher, Targ, Moore, & Smith, 1998). Usually, prayer is regarded as private and per-

Box 8.3

Case Example

A Latina therapist in private practice says that it is natural for her to pray with her religious Latino clients, although she is reluctant to tell professional colleagues that she does so. What might she fear in terms of judgment from her colleagues? How might her culture influence the inclusion of spiritual practices?

sonal. Various questions arise when considering the ethics of prayer in counseling. What is the difference between prayer and meditation? Is there a reason to keep sacred activities separate from the secular?

These are issues that are open for discussion. There are questions of boundaries (e.g., what is the counselor's role and expertise?), client welfare, sacred versus secular, and beliefs and expectations of clients. Various counseling interventions have adapted meditation techniques (e.g., visualization, focused breathing). Suggesting prayer in a counseling session is controversial due to the inherent power imbalances and the risk of the counselor imposing his or her religious values on the client. Discussion of prayer in counseling is included in the next chapter, on spiritual interventions. Mental health professionals tend to be conservative about using prayer in session, but might include clients in their personal prayers. One way a pastoral counselor dealt with this issue was by not initiating prayer with his clients, but if they asked, he invited them to lead it (D. Horn, personal communication, February 9, 1997). He preferred that clients lead because their prayers revealed their concerns more accurately than he could anticipate them. (See Box 8.3.)

Contraindications

Bullis (1996) described situations in which spiritual interventions were contraindicated. He suggested that the clinician be able to differentiate between spiritual concerns and mental illness. Persons who are actively psychotic (e.g., hallucinating or dealing with unwelcome imagery) should not be encouraged to experience spiritual imagery. Second, persons who have been abused by clergy or religious leaders (as well as cult abuse survivors) may be retraumatized by spiritual imagery. Persons who have "had negative spiritual experiences, are undergoing spiritual conversion, are changing spiritual orientations under family duress or other stress, or are undergoing spiritual stress compounded by other types of stress may be overwhelmed by spiritual imagery" (Bullis, 1996, p. 121).

If clients tolerate or respond to spiritual references, they may be able to benefit from further discussion. However, if they respond with stress, such interventions may be contraindicated. Finally, clinicians should respect a client's wishes not to discuss religious or spiritual concerns.

References

Bullis, R. K. (1996). *Spirituality in social work practice.* Washington, DC: Taylor & Francis.

Cornett, C. (1998). *The soul of psychotherapy: Recapturing the spiritual dimension in the therapeutic encounter.* New York: Free Press.

Cortright, B. (1997). *Psychotherapy and spirit: Theory and practice in transpersonal psychotherapy.* Albany: State University of New York Press.

Ganje-Fling, M. A., & McCarthy, P. (1996). Impact of childhood sexual abuse on client spiritual development: Counseling implications. *Journal of Counseling and Development, 74,* 253-258.

Gelso, C. J., & Carter, J. A. (1985). The relationship in counseling and psychotherapy. *The Counseling Psychologist, 13*(5), 155-243.

Hart, M., Stevens, J., & Lieberman, F. (1990). *Drumming at the edge of magic: A journey into the spirit of percussion.* San Francisco: HarperSanFrancisco.

Healey, B. J. (1990). Self-disclosure in religious spiritual direction: Antecedents and parallels to self-disclosure in psychotherapy. In G. Stricker & M. Fisher (Eds.), *Self-disclosure in the therapeutic relationship* (pp. 17-27). New York: Plenum.

Kelly, E. W. (1995). *Spirituality and religion in counseling and psychotherapy: Diversity in theory and practice.* Alexandria, VA: American Counseling Association.

Korb, M. (1988). The numinous ground: I-Thou in gestalt work. *The Gestalt Journal, 11*(1), 97-106.

May, G. G. (1988). *Addiction and grace.* New York: Harper & Row.

Richards, P. S., & Bergin, A. E. (1997). *A spiritual strategy for counseling and psychotherapy.* Washington, DC: American Psychological Association.

School guidelines on religion. (1995). *Christian Century, 112,* 839.

Sicher, F., Targ, E., Moore, D., & Smith, H. S. (1998). A randomized double-blind study of the effect of distant healing in a population with advanced AIDS. *Western Journal of Medicine, 169*(6), 356-363.

Simpkinson, A. A., & Simpkinson, C. H. (1998). *Soul work: A field guide for spiritual seekers.* New York: HarperCollins.

Strupp, H. H., & Binder, J. L. (1984). *Psychotherapy in a new key: A guide to time limited dynamic psychotherapy.* New York: Basic Books.

Tan, S. Y. (1996). Religion in clinical practice: Implicit and explicit integration. In E. P. Shafranske (Ed.), *Religion and the clinical practice of psychology* (pp. 365-387). Washington, DC: American Psychological Association.

9

An Integrative Model and Spiritual Interventions

Why is the search for spirituality so compelling, yet so complicated and difficult? A poem by Rumi, a 13th-century Sufi mystic, reveals some truths about the spiritual journey.

STORY WATER

A story is like water
that you heat for your bath.
It takes messages between the fire
and your skin. It lets them meet,
and it cleans you!
Very few can sit down,
in the middle of the fire itself
like a salamander or Abraham.
We need intermediaries.
A feeling of fullness comes,
but usually it takes some bread
to bring it.
Beauty surrounds us,
but usually we need to be walking

in a garden to know it.
The body itself is a screen
to shield and partially reveal
the light that's blazing
inside your presence.
Water, stories, the body,
all the things we do, are mediums
that hide and show what's hidden.
Study them,
and enjoy this being washed
with a secret we sometimes know,
and then not.

—Coleman Barks (Translator), *The Essential Rumi,* 1995, New York: HarperCollins.

In this final chapter, we will present material aimed at formulating an integrative model for psychological, multicultural, and spiritual growth. By this, we mean that we believe that psychological development is intricately linked to spiritual evolution, and vice versa. In parallel fashion, we suggest that ongoing multicultural work deepens one's spirituality, and vice versa. We will discuss approaches to integrating spiritual interventions into multicultural counseling. Finally, we offer suggestions toward a paradigm shift within the profession to facilitate these changes. We intend this chapter to be a stimulus for "contemplation" and dialogue both within one's self and with others, from which practitioners may formulate their own understandings and refinements based on who they are and the clients with whom they work.

Integrative Model

What is a model for both spiritual and psychological health in a multicultural context? Fortunato (1982) proposed a model for psychological and spiritual growth by using an analogy of a DNA molecule, a double helix:

> One strand of the double spiral represents the psychological or ego dimension; the other strand, the spiritual dimension. Like the DNA molecule, there are a series of links between the two strands. . . . The journey's progress is initiated on the psychic strand as some chunk of the ego is affirmed, and then achieves fruition by jumping across one of the links to the spiritual strand, as that chunk of ego is transcended. (pp. 22-23)

Fortunato (1982) also discussed the relationship between psychological growth and spiritual growth. Therapy and psychological development focus traditionally on self-consciousness, personal control, self-determination, ego development, and autonomy. In spiritual formation, the primary focus is on "enlightenment," pure consciousness, love of God, and union with God. This is accompanied by surrender of the ego and emptying of self in surrender to an all-powerful, ultimate source. Psychology is concerned with self in relation to self. Spirituality is concerned with transcending self and opening to the cosmos (God, Mystery, Ground of Being, or the Sacred). Therein lies a process of both strengthening the ego and giving up the ego.

In a similar fashion, Rubin (1996) has analyzed the parallel streams, confluence, and points of departure of Buddhism and psychoanalysis. He suggested that both traditions have merit but neither alone provides a complete picture of human evolution. Psychoanalysis offers interpretations of psychological defenses and resistances that may impede the opening of one's consciousness through meditation. Buddhism offers a model that exceeds the psychoanalytic frame of reference. A psychotherapist's training offers insights about transferential and countertransferential issues that come up in both the counselor-client relationship and the teacher-student relationship. Spiritual teachers need this insight into these interpersonal dynamics to avoid boundary violations. These two traditions offer complementary perspectives even while they have significant differences. Although psychoanalysis focuses on strengthening the ego and Buddhism focuses on transcending the ego, it can be said that both strengthening of self and letting go of self are important for psychological well-being.

In a holistic model, mind, body, and spirit have equal footing and are intimately connected with each other. We suggest that the double helix model of ego and spirit is a scientific reframing of ancient knowledge; that is, human beings have a spiritual source and wear sociopsychological masks. Since people need culture for survival, this larger context influences perceptions, beliefs, and practices. Therefore, a model that tries fully to capture human growth, development, and change needs to incorporate all of these elements.

We propose an integrative model that builds bridges between psychology and spirituality, between spirituality and multiculturalism, and between various movements within psychology. A logical extension of this model will be to build bridges among various disciplines that are concerned with the well-being of the human condition, such as religion, health sciences, anthropology, and others.

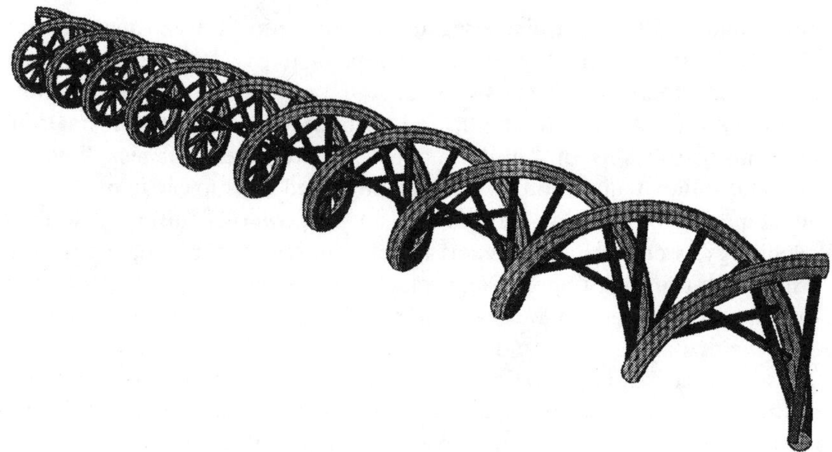

Figure 9.1.

Borrowing from Fortunato and from Rubin, we have visualized a DNA molecule in which spirit and matter interact in a snakelike fashion and weave within a larger context of culture and multicultural perspectives (see Figure 9.1). One dimension does not exist without the other, although consciousness about this process varies significantly. As one develops psychologically (intellectually, socially, physically), these dimensions affect one's expression of spirit. Concurrently, as one's spiritual life is "quickened," psychological issues may come up and need attention. The dance of ego development and ego surrender in life's journeys ultimately enhances the process of spiritual awakening, however difficult this process may be emotionally.

In parallel fashion, multiculturalism and spirituality are intimately interlocked, coming together and coming apart at various points. The interaction of these forces was described in Chapter 4; for example, the values of cultural conflict and cultural differences, flexibility and faith, grace and humor, paradox and bicultural perspectives. We suggest that the ego-spirit "dance" takes place in the larger context of a multicultural community, which informs both internal processes and interactions with others.

Professionals who are committed to multicultural awareness (see the framework for multicultural competency in Chapter 4) will find that tapping into a spiritual river will help nourish and replenish their energies and strengthen them for further challenges. This will also give "deeper" meaning for these experiences. Concurrently, for those committed to a spiritual path, multicultural experiences can be used to stimulate, challenge, and propel them forward (downward, inward, outward) and to expand consciousness, increase compassion, and nurture humor.

Just as the Rumi poem alludes, the multicultural "stories . . . are mediums that hide and show what's hidden" and are potential teachers for the multicultural spiritual seeker. In Chapter 1 we used the example of viewing a movie through 3-D glasses to gain an experience of depth. Similarly, engaging in these multiple processes results in life taking on a deeper dimensionality. Life is felt more fully (senses, body, heart); social issues are as important as personal insights; and, from a holistic perspective, greater connections and caring result both internally and with others.

Integrating Spiritual Interventions

How are spiritual interventions defined and implemented? The "culture" of psychology and counseling usually determines the appropriate behaviors for specific professional roles and relationships. In opening the door to the world of multicultural counseling, we have expanded the possibilities exponentially! In this section, we offer some "process suggestions" for counselors who wish to learn more about spiritual interventions. Then we will describe the "state of the art" of spiritual interventions emerging in the counseling literature. This is currently an area of rapid growth and development in the field, as the parameters of spirituality in counseling continue to be defined. We will conclude this section with a summary of relevant themes for integrating spirituality into multicultural counseling.

First, in terms of process suggestions, we recommend that counselors engage in a study process through which they become clear about their own spiritual and religious beliefs and worldview. This first step will determine the extent to which the spiritual dimension will be integrated into their counseling.

Next, it is natural and perhaps easiest to focus upon the religious or spiritual concerns of the client. Having a knowledge base of how spiritual and religious issues present in multicultural counseling will help counselors to conceptualize and to know their strengths and limitations in addressing these issues. Descriptions of some of these presenting concerns are included in the discussion of spiritual interventions that follows.

Third, we recommend that counselors have a peer supervision group or study group in which these issues can be explored further. In this way, counselors can examine their countertransference issues and can practice and refine their interventions. A multicultural and multidisciplinary group of professionals would be ideal. Such a group needs to be both supportive and challenging in order for the counselor to be able to articulate comfort zones as well as to clarify boundaries.

Finally, we suggest that the degree to which spirituality is integrated into counseling will depend highly upon the individual counselor's spiritual and religious orientation. This could range from an occasional counseling inquiry to a fully integrated therapy style, such as in transpersonal therapy. In addition, the work setting will be an influencing factor. For instance, a secular setting such as a publicly funded institution (e.g., school) may have restrictions on obviously religious practices.

With these suggestions in mind, we will present a brief discussion of spiritual interventions drawn from authors representing the various mental health professions. There are different types of spiritual interventions discussed in the literature, ranging from philosophical positions to concrete behaviors. Interventions range from specific in-session questions or topics to more generally defined theoretical orientations. These research findings indicate some specific parameters on spiritual or religious issues in counseling.

Bullis (1996) surveyed a sample of clinical social workers on the frequency of using spiritual or religious interventions with clients. Respondents who indicated using the intervention with at least 10% of clients were counted as "uses intervention." The most frequently used interventions are listed in Table 9.1. Twenty percent or more of those surveyed used some of these selected interventions. The least used interventions were "performing exorcisms, touching clients for healing purposes, and reading scriptures with clients" (p. 18). These practitioners indicated that they used spiritual interventions more frequently than *religious* interventions.

Richards and Potts (1995) surveyed Mormon psychotherapists on their use of spiritual interventions in psychotherapy. The respondents were asked how frequently they used these interventions and how successful or unsuccessful they were in this endeavor. The authors also discussed case-focused outcome and ethical guidelines for using spiritual interventions. A summary of the most frequently used interventions is in Table 9.2. The least used intervention was "laying on of hands." In addition, therapists thought that the following interventions were inappropriate in psychotherapy: "laying on of hands by the therapist, encouraging clients to

Table 9.1 Most Frequently Used Spiritual Interventions Among Clinical Social Workers

Explore client's spiritual background
Explore client's religious background
Help clients clarify spiritual values
Recommend participation in spiritual programs (meditation groups, 12-step programs, men's or women's groups)
Use spiritual language or metaphors
Pray privately for client
Explore spiritual elements in dreams
Use or recommend spiritual books

NOTE: From Bullis, 1996, p. 19.

confess, client and therapist in-session prayer and spiritual self-disclosure or modeling" (p. 166). Differences may exist in the spiritual interventions listed in Tables 9.1 and 9.2 in part due to the therapists' spiritual or religious orientation and the extent to which the client's spiritual or religious orientation is known.

Predoctoral internship training directors for APA-accredited counseling and clinical psychology internship sites were asked how important they viewed training in the area of religious and spiritual issues (RSI; Golston, Savage, & Cohen, 1998). Approximately one half (n = 210, 48%) of training directors responded to a mail-out survey that asked about training practices and learning goals for this topic area. Of the respondents, 71, or 34%, indicated that they did some training in this area, typically through clinical supervision, seminars, guest speakers, or a combination of these. The number of sites reporting training activities were led by college counseling centers, followed by medical and VA hospitals. The top-rated items that indicated goals of training are in Table 9.3.

The least endorsed items of these training goals were "learning how to appropriately discuss one's own religious/spiritual belief system with clients" and "learning how to use specific religious/spiritual practices (e.g., prayer, scripture reading) in therapy sessions." A factor analysis yielded five factors grouped as follows: (a) clinical implications of religion/spirituality, (b) religious/spiritual self-awareness, (c) general

Table 9.2 Spiritual Interventions Most Frequently Used by Mormon Psychotherapists

Therapist silent prayer (in-session)
Teaching spiritual or religious concepts
Encouraging forgiveness
Use of religious community as an extra-therapy resource
Encouraging client private prayers

NOTE: From Richards & Potts, 1995, p. 165.

Table 9.3 Top-Rated Goals of Training Items From a Survey of Internship Training Practices Regarding Religious/Spiritual Issues (RSI)

Becoming aware of ethical issues in supervising counselors in training who have specific religious beliefs (e.g., views on homosexuality, abortion, etc.)
Becoming aware of one's religious/spiritual biases
Becoming aware of limitations in one's competency in dealing with religious/spiritual issues (RSI) in therapy
Becoming sensitized to religion/spirituality as a component of clients' cultural contexts
Becoming aware of stereotypes one holds related to particular religious/spiritual traditions or adherents
Becoming aware of how one's own religious/spiritual belief system may influence the counseling process
Becoming aware of the role of religion and spirituality for special populations (i.e., ethnicity, disability, sexual orientation, sex, age)
Becoming aware of one's own religious/spiritual values
Becoming aware of RSI as aspects of presenting issues in therapy (e.g., death of a loved one, low self-esteem, depression, relationship issues, feelings of guilt)
Learning to assess the role of RSI in client pathology
Learning when and how to refer clients to religious leaders for spiritual counseling or consultation
Increasing counselor comfort level and skill in raising and dealing with RSI

NOTE: From Golston, Savage, & Cohen, 1998.

knowledge of religion or spirituality, (d) engaging clients' religious or spiritual beliefs, and (e) idiographic aspects of religion or spirituality.

Golston and colleagues (1998) have identified specific types of interventions that may be useful in a general sense in counseling. These interventions may also be linked to specific content issues, such as grief work, search for meaning, recovery from trauma or addictions, and others. Beyond specific religious or spiritual interventions as described above, there are counseling approaches that are more or less integrative of spirituality.

Westgate (1996) identified specific counseling approaches that integrate a spiritual dimension. The work of Hinterkopf (1994, 1997) utilized a focusing technique that invites a "larger perspective" on specific problems. She advised counselors to attend training workshops before introducing this technique into their practice. Other approaches included psychosynthesis (Ferrucci, 1982) and other interventions like dream work (Halligan & Shea, 1991), use of metaphors, meditation, guided imagery, and breath work (see Scotton, Chinen, & Battista, 1996).

It seems important to conceptualize the use of spiritual interventions based on certain criteria in order to avoid a "cookbook" of interventions with clients or a random selection of exercises. We suggest exploring some of the following questions and themes as therapy proceeds:

First, and foremost, it is important to make sure that interventions are "grounded" in the genuineness of the counselor and the reality of the client, bearing in mind all of the luggage the counseling profession offers (for an extensive discussion of theories and techniques, see Kelly, 1995). It is important to base interventions on information from the general assessment and, specifically, any spiritual and religious assessments conducted with the client. Multiculturally, it is important to pay attention to within-group differences of clients who might otherwise be stereotyped through cultural group membership; for example, determining the stage of identity development of a client. Obviously not all people from any one group are alike, and yet the tendency is for counselors to apply certain techniques and approaches to cultural group members because they worked with one member of that group before. In short, as a colleague once put it, it is important to learn all the "book" knowledge about a cultural group, then set it back on the shelf (keeping it close by) and start over when working with an individual in therapy (J. Dowis, personal communication, October 11, 1998).

Second, it is helpful to be aware of the full "canvas" of the presenting issues in counseling. Chapters 6 and 7 discussed certain content issues directly related to spirituality and multiculturalism. It is important to understand fully how these issues are "real" for clients, how clients experience these issues day to day, and how these issues are similar to others and how they are different. It is also important for counselors to be knowledgeable about certain typical presenting issues and to feel comfortable, first, in understanding the painting, and then in reworking the canvas with the client.

Third, counselors need to be aware of how spirituality can help address certain content issues and to know when it is contraindicated (see discussion in Chapter 8).

Fourth, it is important for counselors to be aware of their own spirituality and to assess their own place in their spiritual journey (see Chapters 2 and 3 for models of spiritual worldviews and development).

Fifth, it is important for counselors to be aware of their own development in multiculturalism and of their own identity. We refer readers back to Chapter 4 for personal reflections on these processes.

Sixth, it is important for counselors to be aware of clients' support systems when working with clients to make changes. These support systems may include spiritual teachers or guides, religious personnel, friends, and family. It may even be relevant to suggest multidimensional types of support, including people who can challenge, people who can give emotional support, people who can give praise, and people who can listen. Seashore (1984) provided a conceptualization for different types of support, including challenge, support, emotional nurturing, and practical advice. It is important to sustain these support systems because growth and change require multidimensional support (i.e., different types of support for different times in one's life; not expecting all support to come from one source; and learning how to ask for support).

Seventh, be aware of multicultural theory and practice in counseling, and continue developing skills in how to integrate these perspectives and techniques (see review of literature in Chapter 1).

Paradigm Shift

As a final section in this book, we suggest that there needs to be a paradigm shift that will facilitate change toward a holistic model of mental health that integrates the spiritual dimension. Futurists have talked about the need for new models to cope with a postmodern world, and such visionary thinking is seeping into the counseling literature. Hansen

(1997) has integrated a holistic approach to career development, and O'Hara (1998) has suggested that gestalt therapy may be useful as a transformational psychology for contemporary shifts in human consciousness. For example, she suggests that in a postmodern world we need "creative pluralism, mutual recognition, diversity with tolerance, dynamic stability, contained competition, and collaboration" (p. 158).

We suggest that bridges need to be built as part of an integrative model of psychological and spiritual health. More concretely, we suggest that people need intentionally to dialogue with each other, where heretofore little exchange has taken place. For example, professors in the University of Florida Religion Department have joined forces with interested faculty in the School of Medicine to examine the relationship between spirituality and healing (S. Isenberg, personal communication, December 3, 1998). In addition to discussion across disciplines, such as religion, anthropology, sociology, and others, we suggest that there needs to be more intradisciplinary dialogue, such as among the various movements within psychology. As an example, what can the transpersonalists learn from the psychologists who study religion, and vice versa? In addition, mental health professionals need to communicate across professional boundaries through interdisciplinary forums. Such dialogues can be nurtured by following multicultural guidelines and spiritual values delineated in Chapter 4.

In addition, we suggest that the process of "discernment" be applied to groups and community settings when striving for group harmony. With so much focus on individualism in the United States, it is necessary to balance this by paying attention to the "higher good" of the group or community as well.

As cultural diversity becomes a lived reality, alternative healing modalities will be seen as credible and valuable in a pluralistic society. Counselors, psychologists, and social workers may refer equally to acupuncturists, herbalists, indigenous healers, psychiatrists, or therapeutic massage therapists, depending upon the appropriateness for clients (Sue & Sue, 1998).

We encourage members of the mental health professions to be active participants in creating new paradigms for learning and living in the 21st century. We offer some thoughts by contrasting old and new models of ways of being in Table 9.4, but suggest that the real value of pursuing new paradigms will come when these are created and enacted at the grassroots level.

Table 9.4 Contrasting Models

Old Model	*New Model*
Competition for limited resources	Unlimited spiritual source & multicultural opportunities
Specialization & reductionism	Holism, cross-discipline discussions, intradiscipline dialogues
Fragmentation	Integration
Secular/religious split	Open dialogue
Religious intolerance	Religious tolerance is promoted
Values free counseling	Values clarified
Religion as exclusive	Religion as inclusive
Domination & hierarchy	Partnerships & allies
Survival of own group	Survival of planet

Conclusion

This book has been written about the intersection of counseling, spirituality, and multicultural awareness from a psychological perspective. Just as many authors have framed spirituality from a psychological worldview, we have approached it with the following primary values: humanistic valuing of people, developmental perspectives, mindfulness, ultimate valuing of multiple worldviews as a means for expansion of consciousness and consequent spiritual awareness, and an emphasis on the process dimension of engaging in spirituality and multiculturalism.

Unlike the study of psychological theory, we do not believe it is possible to understand or transmit understanding of spirituality without some experiential base. We therefore invite those who desire further understanding of spirituality to engage at the appropriate level for self in activities that support, nurture, and expand their individual bases of understanding. Just as in multicultural awareness processes, reading is one level (knowledge), but without personal awareness and life experience it becomes an intellectual exercise without real import. Multiculturally and spiritually speaking, true empathy is accomplished by "walking in another person's shoes" across cultures.

In closing, we ask you to engage in a process and a journey of beginning, or continuing, to formulate your own answers to the following questions, preferably in collaboration with personal and professional peers:

What aspects of multicultural and spiritual awareness, knowledge, and skills do you anticipate integrating into your counseling practice, whether at the personal awareness level, in the counseling relationship, or as spiritual interventions?

Where is your comfort zone in bringing up or responding to religious/spiritual/transpersonal issues in therapy?

Where is your boundary: That is, when might you refer a client or decline to engage in a discussion about a specific issue or processes?

What other questions are you ready to explore?

References

Barks, C. (Trans.). (1995). *The essential Rumi.* New York: HarperCollins.

Bullis, R. K. (1996). *Spirituality in social work practice.* Washington, DC: Taylor & Francis.

Ferrucci, P. (1982). *What we may be: Techniques for psychological and spiritual growth through psychosynthesis.* Los Angeles, CA: Tarcher.

Fortunato, J. E. (1982). *Embracing the exile: Healing journeys of gay Christians.* New York: Harper & Row.

Golston, S. S., Savage, J. S., & Cohen, G. (1998, August). *Internship training practices regarding religious and spiritual issues.* Paper presented at the 106th Annual Convention of the American Psychological Association, San Francisco.

Halligan, F. R., & Shea, J. J. (1991). Sacred images in dreamwork: The journey into self as journey into God. *Pastoral Psychology, 40,* 29-38.

Hansen, L. S. (1997). *Integrative life planning: Critical tasks for career development and changing life patterns.* San Francisco: Jossey-Bass.

Hinterkopf, E. (1994). Integrating spiritual experiences in counseling. *Counseling and Values, 38,* 165-175.

Hinterkopf, E. (1997). *Integrating spirituality in counseling: A manual for using the experiential focusing method.* Alexandria, VA: American Counseling Association.

Kelly, E. W. (1995). *Spirituality and religion in counseling and psychotherapy.* Alexandria, VA: American Counseling Association.

O'Hara, M. (1998). Gestalt therapy as an emancipatory psychology for a transmodern world. *Gestalt Review, 2,* 154-168.

Scotton, B. W., Chinen, A. B., & Battista, J. R. (Eds.). (1996). *Textbook of transpersonal psychiatry and psychology.* New York: Basic Books.

Seashore, C. (1984). Developing and using a personal support system. In L. Porter & B. Mohr (Eds.), *Reading book for human relations training* (pp. 43-47). Alexandria, VA: NTL Institute.

Sue, D. W., & Sue, D. (1998). *Counseling the culturally different: Theory and practice* (3rd ed.). New York: John Wiley.

Richards, P. S., & Potts, R. W. (1995). Using spiritual interventions in psychotherapy: Practices, successes, failures, and ethical concerns of Mormon psychotherapists. *Professional Psychology: Research and Practice, 26,* 163-170.

Rubin, J. B. (1996). *Psychotherapy and Buddhism: Toward an integration.* New York: Plenum.

Westgate, C. (1996). Spiritual wellness and depression. *Journal of Counseling & Development, 75,* 26-35.

Index

About the Authors

Mary A. Fukuyama works at the University of Florida Counseling Center in Gainesville as a counseling psychologist and is an affiliate clinical professor for the Department of Counselor Education and the Counseling Psychology Program in the Department of Psychology. She teaches on the subject of "spiritual issues in counseling," and has taught courses in career development and multicultural counseling. She is involved in supervision and training with predoctoral interns and practicum students and enjoys being in a work environment that promotes lifelong learning. Her professional interests revolve around a continuing "quest" to investigate and integrate spirituality and multicultural counseling. She is also interested in professional development of mental health professionals over the life span. Originally from the Pacific Northwest, she received her graduate degree from Washington State University, Pullman. She claims a "pioneering spirit" from ancestors on both sides of her family, one root from Japan, the other from Britain. She enjoys travel and most recently has explored Guatemala and Mexico. Her other leisure activities include being with her family and friends, and enjoying canoeing, watercolor, and time at the beach.

Todd D. Sevig received his Ph.D. in counseling psychology from The Ohio State University. Currently, he is a senior assistant director for clinical services at Counseling & Psychological Services and an adjunct lecturer in the Department of Psychology at the University of Michigan. He is also the father of two children, Mara, age 6, and Joseph, age 4, and the son of a former Lutheran minister from Minnesota. His interests involve incorporating spirituality in counseling, working toward multiculturalism in a number of areas including group work, training of trainers, counseling, supervising, and teaching. He has codeveloped a multicultural seminar for psychology/social work interns, been involved in multicultural curriculum development, and for a number of years trained college students in multicultural peer interventions. He has taught or cotaught courses in group facilitation in a multicultural setting, exploring White experiences in a multicultural society and peer approaches to helping. Research interests include examining identity development across social groups (e.g., race, gender, sexual orientation) and integrating multiculturalism and spirituality. When not working, he spends available time involved in writing, playing, and listening to music.